BEING A CREATIVE GENIUS

Gayatri Kalra Sehgal is an accomplished artist. Educating young children, with an engaging dash of creativity, was a new dream for her. She has attended seminars, intensive workshops and exclusive courses on child development, curriculum design, effective communication, train the trainer, etc., helping her understand the specific requirements of children.

She has set up a Day Care Centre and two schools, first as the principal and later as a dean, and carefully designed the academic curricula. She has innovated and revolutionized a novel way of writing the report cards called 'Child's Intelligence Profile.'

Presently, she conducts seminars for distinguished educators and creates awareness among parents of differently abled children. This workbook is an extensive collection of her experiences and vision to create global leaders for tomorrow. She has also authored *Winning Strategies for Parents*, *SUPER CHILD! Unlocking the Secrets of Working Memory*, *Being a Brilliant Thinker: Mastering Intelligent Thinking Skills* and *Being a Mathematician: Mastering Secrets of Mental Math*.

SKILLS THAT BUILD

BEING A CREATIVE GENIUS

Mastering Activities That Inspire Creativity

Gayatri Kalra Sehgal

RUPA

Published by
Rupa Publications India Pvt. Ltd 2019
7/16, Ansari Road, Daryaganj
New Delhi 110002

Sales Centres:

Allahabad Bengaluru Chennai
Hyderabad Jaipur Kathmandu
Kolkata Mumbai

ISBN: 978-93-5333-480-2

First impression 2019

10 9 8 7 6 5 4 3 2 1

Printed by HT Media Ltd, Gr. Noida

To my sons,

Divyamshu and Kuber

Contents

ATTENTION

OBSERVATION

ASSOCIATION

Foreword

'Creativity is the key to success in the future, and primary education is where teachers can bring creativity in children at that level,' said Dr A.P.J. Abdul Kalam. On similar lines, Gayatri Kalra Sehgal, with her vision to create global leaders for tomorrow, concentrates on 'Developing a Creative Child' based on her extensive experiences. This resulted in her writing this book.

Creativity, basically, is the ability to produce original ideas and new items. Three major components of creativity are: the creative person, the creative product and the creative process. Creativity in children has to be carefully developed and nurtured to transform them into creative people. The fact that children are truly creative is due to the spontaneity in their actions and reactions. This aspect of fostering creativity has been dealt with in the book by Gayatri. She has given useful guidelines for the parents to lead their children towards divergent thought and master creativity.

I whole-heartedly endorse *Being a Creative Genius: Mastering Activities That Inspire Creativity* by Gayatri Kalra Sehgal and recommend that the procedures in the book may be followed in every school by the teachers and in every home by the parents because today's children are tomorrow's future.

Anshul B. Sharma
Chairman, Shastri Group of Institutes

Introduction

Engineer the Idea

The beautiful world we see around is the result of ingenuity, perseverance and creativity of geniuses, especially our engineers, technologists and scientists. We owe a lot to them.

Let me begin by giving you a few examples.

Charles Goodyear accidentally dropped rubber gum and Sulphur on the stove. The result obtained was a hard black material. This is how vulcanized rubber was invented!

Blotting paper was invented by accident when a worker forgot to put emulsion on the surface of the paper to smoothen it.

However, the question remains—can the invention of vulcanized rubber be termed as creativity? No, it was created by accident! This accident gave birth to an idea. Ideas are available a dime a dozen, but the most daunting task is to engineer the idea and convert it into a product, which can be put to use!

Hence, 'creative processes' began when vulcanized rubber was used to manufacture various products, which were useful and created value.

Let us understand what 'creativity' really means.

Creativity, as defined by dictionaries, refers to 'the ability to create'. However, this definition is somewhat incomplete.

Creativity refers to the ability of the curious mind to identify knowledge and information from different and unrelated sources, and make connections and associations between them, which will lead to the formation of perceptions that generates novel solutions to be used.

Curious Is the New Brave

Curiosity is the compelling force of a constantly hungry mind. Creativity has its roots in curiosity. Curiosity introduces a new dimension to creativity.

A curious mind constantly seeks food for thought. To satisfy its hunger, the brain constantly explores and seeks acquisition of primary facts to develop tangible solutions.

Curiosity could be about anything—yourself, the world around you or even the daily choices you make. It helps enhance the quality of life by improving awareness and developing more nuanced perspectives. A creative 'change' in the thought process brings beauty to life.

The reason why children are 'truly creative' is that they are spontaneous in their actions and reactions. Children are at their 'maximum level of creativity' in conducive environments, and they grow into happy adaptable human beings. However, to be curious, one needs to be brave—brave enough to overlook the regimented norms, break the conventions and grow 'beyond' their abilities. It takes a brave heart to sieve criticism and only take in those that will help people evolve into creative beings.

Creative Perception

As key facilitators, when we respond appropriately to the creative interests of young children, answer their questions and cater to their energy levels, we give them a multitude of opportunities to grow into sound adults. Facilitate and enthusiastically support the children when they are experiencing a 'creative moment'*.

---

*A creative moment is the time when the child is at his or her maximum

Remember that the best time to provide guidance is not when facilitators feel like it is the right time to do so, but the time when the child is experiencing a creative moment. Then and only then the creative perception in him or her begins to develop rapidly.

Children are creative, and age has a negligible role to play. Creativity only enhances with time and practice. Guard your child from the negativity in society if you wish him or her to evolve into his or her own identity.

Blame Michelangelo!

Over the centuries, Michelangelo has been considered as the God of Creativity. Unfortunately, for most, creativity is all about equating their work with that of the most eminent people in the world. Similarly, well-meaning adults try to encourage children by comparing their child's work with that of the young Michelangelo! This notion creates a psychological barrier in the minds of many children. These psychological barriers result in unfortunate lack of interest in creativity and mar the curiosity in the child, leading to poor confidence. This gives rise to the 'I can't do it' thought process in children. This becomes inadvertently the most common factor why people reluctantly withdraw from being creative. Guard your child against it. **Remember that:**

Creativity never dies.

It just becomes dormant in a hostile environment.

It springs back to life through proper motivation and guidance.

Michelangelo is history! We do not need more of

---

level of creativity. When the child is experiencing a 'creative moment', he or she is open to absorb maximum information and associate it with the existing information in his or her memory to come up with new and innovative ideas.

Michelangelos.

We need people of the present era to bring in creativity that is unique in nature and will last in the years to come.

'The Ghost' That Haunts Creativity

Here is a list, which will help us understand why children (or even adults) withdraw from being creative.

- Fear of 'beginning' or 'never done this' attitude
- Lack of inspiration
- Lack of commitment
- Comparison with the next-door 'Michelangelo'
- Self-doubt
- Fear of rejection
- Parent(s) or teacher(s) won't appreciate it
- Nobody in the class has tried it yet
- Fear of becoming a laughing stock

Children seek acceptance and appreciation, and the fear of being wrong or rejected causes stress in young creative minds. Offering the security of being accepted and appreciated, when they share their creative work with their parents, makes children happy. This costs nothing, but the positive gesture from the parents helps to create a genius in the years to come. To help a creative being evolve, it is the 'seed' of acceptance and encouragement that needs to be sowed and nurtured at all times.

Here, I would like to reinforce a note from my previous book *Super Child! Unlocking the Secrets of Working Memory* as it holds true for learning creativity as well!

> To facilitate children to succeed in the world that is changing at a rapid pace, we need to keep abreast with the changing trends. The challenges we face are not the

challenges our forthcoming generations will face. However, without knowing the changes the future is going to bring in, it becomes imperative for educators and the parents to help children focus on their working memory (creativity).

We need to prepare the children to become successful global leaders of tomorrow by enhancing their working memory at the correct age. Unfortunately, to make such future leaders, we must enhance their required skills, which buckle under academic pressures and narrows down their possibilities to evolve.

The Anchor Points of Creativity

We as parents need to make our children 'future-ready' by enhancing their creativity today. The anchor points of creativity are a set of skills, which business leaders require in potential candidates. Let us understand what the anchor points of creativity offer and the skills required in business leaders.

Anchor Points of Creativity	Required Skills in Business Leaders
Curiosity	Knowledge seeking and an inquisitive mind
Attention	Focus
Observation	Sharp observers
Association	Network
Perception	Cognizant
Understanding knowledge	Manages information
Problem-solving abilities	Solves problems
Good behaviour	Strong work-ethics
Risk takers	Risk takers

Explores and reformulates information	Research
Creativity	Innovation
Transition time	Manages change effectively
Manages stress	Manages stress
Confidence	Confidence
Responsibility	Responsible
Decision-making abilities	Decision-making abilities
Leadership skills	Leadership skills
Team work	Team work
Punctuality	Time management and punctuality
Self-motivation	Go-getters
Self-help	Independent

Learning Outcomes of Creativity

Now that we know the 'anchor points of creativity', let us look at the 'learning outcomes' of creativity.

- Developed curiosity
- Improved attention span
- Enhanced observation
- Helps in seeking and exploring possibilities
- Helps in perceiving the world differently
- Associates and synthesizes information
- Encourages fantasies and imagination
- Identifies freedom of choice and exercises it
- Enhanced decision-making skills
- Ability to form their own hypothesis

- Goal-driven
- Encourages persistence
- Team work and acceptance towards others' views
- Sense of achievement
- Enhanced bilateral coordination
- Enhanced personal, social and emotional skills
- Enhanced empathy, self-esteem and self-confidence
- Physical Development–gross motor and fine motor skills
- Enhanced sensory skills
- Developed communication skills (language, vocabulary, speaking and listening skills)
- Developed meta-cognition skills
- Numeracy skills
- Developed reasoning skills
- Inculcates self-discipline
- Helps in letting out their energies and calming down

Understanding Creativity in Children

As conscious parents and facilitators, we need to motivate and inspire children towards creativity. Children are curious and possess ubiquitous interests; once the child feels inspired and begins showing curiosity, he or she begins to pay attention to the subject at hand. The child subsequently begins to form associations by using different unrelated objects to create new things; the creativity of a child begins to evolve, and hence, can be monitored.

However, to carefully monitor the development of creativity in a child, parents or facilitators should possess the required skilled efforts to identify, understand and facilitate his or her divergent thinking. Most often, I have seen, that it is the level of parents' or facilitators' understanding of the child's interest(s) that is amiss and he or she inevitably gets the label of being uninterested in learning. For example, several times, in visually stimulating areas such as shopping malls—where the merchandise is displayed in the most visually appealing manner—children are seen walking with their arms and hands spread out, trying to touch everything that comes within their reach. It is challenging and strenuous for concerned parents and facilitators to manage such behaviour due to various reasons at 'our level'. However, if we look at it from the child's perspective or 'their level', the child is naturally trying to observe and experience information using their sense organs and is taking risks to explore his or her boundaries.

Mentioned below is the 'Wheel of Creativity' that explains the links and process of developing creativity in a child. If the child demonstrates a lack of interest in any sphere, where creativity is required, check the weak link and begin 'work' from there. For example, if the child is not paying 'attention' on the given task, check for the previous link—curiosity—and begin by developing it (curiosity about the subject in this case) such that it catches the 'attention' of the child in a way that he or she begins to 'observe' information. The child will then begin to form 'strong associations', which enhances the way he or she forms perceptions. Clearer perceptions lead to the development of skills and the child is able to create novel solutions that can be put to use and make the surroundings not just beautiful but also purposeful.

The Wheel of Creativity

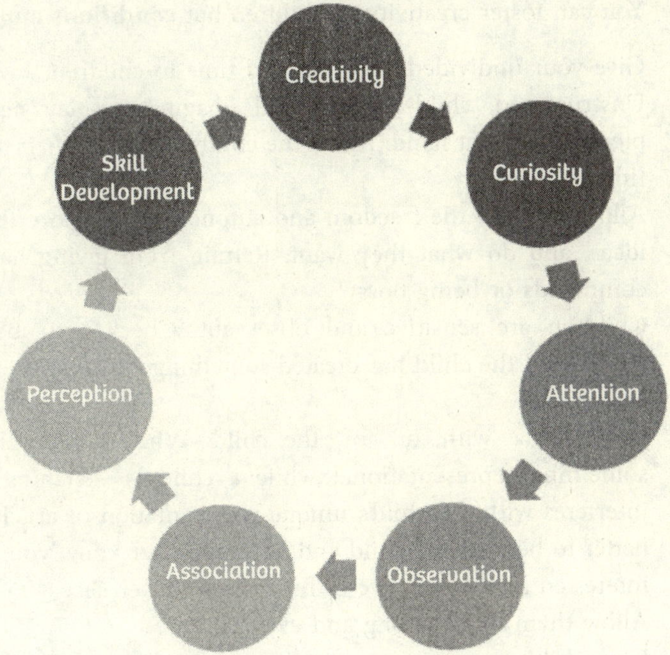

Merging Creativity with Learning

An important question that arises is: How can facilitators gracefully merge creativity with learning to enhance and channelize a child's curiosity, which will develop their attention into productive and generative creativity?

To answer this, we first need to understand that 'creativity' is a process and not a destination for the child! The priority should be to help the child enjoy the process of the creative experience. Once the child begins to enjoy the process, learning will automatically take place! 'Pied Piper' or the facilitator can then drive the learning into a new dimension of a learning experience and only then, creativity can be facilitated and then fostered!

You can foster creativity in children but **conditions apply!**

1. Give your undivided attention and time to children.
2. Unstructured, child-directed and imaginative play needs plenty of time at hand. Allow the children to take *their own* time to play.
3. Allow children the freedom and autonomy to explore their ideas, and do what they want. Refrain from giving harsh commands or being bossy!
4. Children are sensitive and observant. Check your body language if the child has created something that you do not approve of.
5. Don't draw 'with' or 'for' the child. When adults draw something representational while a child is sketching, it interferes with the child's unique representation of art. It is better to be near the child and let him or her know you are interested and supportive of his or her masterpiece.
6. Allow them to go wrong and even fail.
7. Give children many opportunities and respect to express 'divergent thought'. Allow them to disagree and debate.
8. Allow the child to contradict and let the child reflect on his or her artwork. When the child does so—attempts to discover the possibility of mistakes and then corrects them—it creates the required 'shift' in the mindset of the child. This shift works as the key catalyst and the child strives for a higher level of perfection.
9. Refrain from giving incentives to children for exhibiting creativity. Incentives interfere with the creative process. It reduces the quality of their responses and the flexibility of their thoughts. Reward the child by asking about the process

of making the masterpiece. Express your curiosity and interest in their learning experiences. Genuinely compliment their improvements.

10. If the child feels that the artwork is 'complete', it is complete! A completed piece of art gives the child a sense of satisfaction and achievement. The child has worked hard on it and has rightly completed it. Do not direct them to make changes and take away the moment from him or her. However, suggest improvements, if required, with respect towards the subsequent creative work.

Creative Environment

Mentioned below are two different approaches of providing children with a 'resourceful learning environment':

1. To conveniently create a resourceful learning environment at home, foster creativity in and outside the study environment, mark separate sections of the house for focussed learning outcomes. For example, keep the living room for social interactions and developing communication skills. Every time you have guests at home, invite the child to socialize and communicate with them. Later, discuss the strategies of effective communication with children at their level. Bedrooms are for leisure; lobbies are for social science conversations; the veranda is for environmental science; the kitchen is for mathematics, and so on. These markings are 'only for parents and facilitators' to consciously demarcate, as it helps us remember and discuss relevant topics. Once the facilitator has learned the trick, the marked learning sections will blend naturally into children.
2. Provide 'adequate' resources required for creative expression. As a facilitator, intermittently remove all the learning aids or

toys from the environment. Instead, provide them with plenty of recyclable materials (a short list of recyclable material has been provided later in this chapter). As a facilitator, only facilitate the children while they perceive knowledge and information from diverse and unrelated materials. The children then are able to subsequently make new connections and associations to generate novel solutions that they could play with. I have seen my students engineer a toy train using recyclable materials such as shoe boxes, bottle lids, broomsticks and ropes! I have witnessed my students using corrugated cardboard sheets and bottle caps to make castanets and weighing scales using cloth hangers, ropes and dishes. They used different types of stones to make different shapes and forms and not merely using pre-set games, educational aids to make different shapes!

Need for Eco-centric Approach to Creativity

It is important for the present generation to like and understand the concept and the significance of 'recycling'. We need to encourage and support children so that they appreciate and care for the environment in the years to come. There is a pressing need to inculcate a sense of 'belonging' to the earth and being 'eco-centric'.

Parents want to provide the best of everything—expensive toys and playing equipment—to their children. The question arises: Is there 'everything right' about providing the best of everything to children at all times? Is there a need for us to 'rethink'? In our endeavours to provide the best of everything to children, are we taking away 'something'? Let us scratch the surface and look deeper at the more meaningful aspects of 'recycling'.

Recycling helps children to learn how to live within the means available and to create something new using unrelated objects.

For example, when children create houses by using the recyclable material, such as shoeboxes and hay, they visualize unrelated materials to create the house. It gives them the opportunity to 'associate' and build on their imagination. On the other hand, if we provide everything readymade to children, such as expensive toys, they will play with them for a while and then forget about them only to create a mess to clear later. However, when we provide recyclable material to children, they begin the creative journey and combine diverse things that can be used. They look at their work as a masterpiece and develop self-esteem and self-confidence in their work.

Most of the things available around us can be utilized for recreational purposes. However, we should help children choose material that is safe for them.

Discuss with children the reasons why certain objects are dangerous, and avoid using acid containers, battery waste, materials with sharp and rusted edges, as these materials may not be safe for the children.

List of Recyclable Materials

Here are a few things readily available at home, which can be creatively recycled:

- Paper
  - Office paper
  - White or coloured paper
  - Newspaper
  - Magazines
  - Greeting cards
  - Catalogues
  - Phonebooks
  - Paperboard

- Heavy-weight folders
- Paper towels and toilet paper rolls
- Food packaging (unwaxed)
- Books (paperbacks and hardbacks)
- Paper bags
- Bubble wraps

- Cartons, cans and containers
  - Tissue boxes
  - Juice and soy milk cartons
  - Cardboard
  - Corrugated cardboard
  - Cereal boxes
  - Shoeboxes

- Metal and tin beverage containers
  - Metal and tin food containers
  - Aluminium foil
  - Aluminium pie plates and trays

- Kitchen cookware
  - Pots, pans, tins and utensils
  - Glasses
  - Lids
  - Plastic cups
  - Screw top jars
  - Milk jugs
  - Soap bottles
  - Laundry detergent boxes

- Old clothes
  - T-shirts
  - Pants and jeans
  - Bed sheets and pillow covers

- Kitchen napkins, placemats, rugs
- Old curtains
- Sofa covers

The list of resources can go on forever as long as we use our 'associative creativity'.

When Creativity becomes Sustainable

Advantages of learning creativity through recycling:

1. Recycling not only helps to reduce waste but also tickles creative skills in children.
2. It will help the future generations to keep the planet green and safe and conserve natural resources, such as water, save energy, and reduce gas emissions that contribute to global climate change.
3. By encouraging children to recycle material in creative ways, they will become future-ready.
4. It enhances associative creativity, which will lead to generative creativity and help sustain resources and beauty.

Remember to Remember

When I conduct seminars on creativity, a lot of parents ask me this question: What are the things that a Nobel prize winner or a very successful person does differently than others? I tell them the facts mentioned below, which I would like to share with you here.

1. *Strong parental support:*

   Instill faith in your child. Give your child the opportunity to challenge his or her limits and be better than his or her own self rather than in comparison with the peers. When the child feels that the parents are positive and appreciative about the efforts and improvements made by the child, he or she begins to develop self-confidence and attempts to take risks. Unflinching support is the magic that has never failed the test of time. Support the child and wait for the magic to happen!

2. *Encourage the child to play a musical instrument or play a sport:*
   Children are overly burdened with academic pressure, and the schools underestimate the importance of integrating extracurricular activities into the curriculum. However, the question arises: Why must a child be introduced and encouraged to choose at least one extracurricular activity as a hobby?

   The human brain has two hemispheres, namely the 'right' and the 'left' hemispheres. Each hemisphere demonstrates its expertise in its defined areas. Allowing the child to pursue learning an instrument, such as drums, or playing a sport, such as swimming, ensures that he or she uses all his or her limbs simultaneously. This means that both the hemispheres have to function at their optimum level to achieve the desired results. The more the two hemispheres learn to sync and coordinate their functions, the better is the learning capacity of the child. As the brain gets habituated to having both the hemispheres of the brain work together for a longer span of time, it develops the required attention and focus to absorb information for an extended span of time. As the attention span begins to be maintained for a longer span of time, it is transformed into achieving higher-grade levels at school.

   The distinguished scientist Albert Einstein is the best example. Einstein learned violin as a child and though he disliked it initially, he later shared the fact that his 'Theory of Relativity' was a 'musical thought' and that, had he not learned violin, he would never have been interested in Physics or invented the theory! Einstein's second wife, Elsa, remarked that playing music helped Einstein to think about theories.

3. *Read and ask questions*:
Reading for or with the child has many known advantages. However, along with reading with the child, also ask 'open-ended' questions. This allows the child to think in creative ways, explore, experiment and infer results. It also helps parents to discover the innermost fears and hidden potentials in their child. Therefore, read and ask as many questions as you can and allow the child to have fun and work on his or her intelligence!

4. *Support originality:*
Encourage the child to leave an impression of not just his or her creativity but also of his or her originality on the coming generations. Remind the child, as often as possible, that we do not need more of Michelangelo, but we do need 'you' and your creative genius to create beautiful things for the future generations to remember.

5. *Inspire a goal-free living* not *a focus-free living:*
For most people, when they have a 'goal', they are able to focus. However, creative people have a unique quality. They prefer to focus on the experience than on the very goal itself. Encourage children to understand that goals are for underachievers. Inspire children to aspire for life-expanding insights and choose quality over quantity, freedom over the limiting goals.

TIP: Only a limiting creative experience arrives at a destination. However, creative people never arrive at a capping destination called the 'goal'. A child can surprise you with his or her capabilities; do not limit them with goals. Remember: 'goal-free' and not 'focus-free' methods.

6. *Think in terms of feelings:*
   Inculcate values in children. Help them to think about their feelings. Make the best use of 'thinking through emotions' as the inner-calling of creativity.

7. *Form opinions:*
   Everybody, including you and I, has opinions, and we strongly believe that our opinions are right. These opinions were formed when we agreed and disagreed upon certain issues. Our opinions help us form unique personalities. Allow the child to disagree and debate over issues. It will give you the best opportunity to encourage the child's thinking in the correct direction.

8. *Working hours for a creative mind:*
   Everybody has a preferred time when they are most creative. Allow the child to work during the hours that work best for him or her.

9. *Unstructured exploration:*
   Give the child time to learn without being interfered by nagging adults. Free time to explore gives wings to the imagination of a creative child. Stop nagging and start enjoying learning with your child.

10. *Self-reflection—the appetizer for creative growth:*
    Guide the child to reflect and be honest with themselves. Encourage them to believe that self-criticism and true self-reflection help evolve creativity and lead to growth and not disappointments.

11. *Fun for intelligence:*
    When the intelligence of the child is mixed with some fun, creativity begins to evolve. Integrate creativity and the element of fun in learning to see how real miracles can be!

    As you facilitate children in their remarkable journey towards creative learning, remember to create fond memories!

Curiosity

Activity–1

The Kaleidoscope!

RESOURCES REQUIRED

- Mirrors, glue gun, sticking tape, foam and coloured beads
- 3 pre-cut equal sized, rectangular mirrors
- Glue gun
- Foam sheet–large enough to wrap around the Kaleidoscope
- 1 masking tape
- 2 coloured tapes
- Plenty of coloured beads
- 1 dish
- A pair of child-safe scissors

Getting Ready:

This activity needs children to use mirrors, which may have sharp edges. So, ensure that you have enough time for supervision.

Method:

1. Invite the children to take three mirrors and place them together to form an equilateral triangle, with the mirrors facing inwards.
2. Using the glue gun, help them stick the edges of the newly-formed triangle. Once the glue has dried up, ask them to

take the foam sheet and wrap it around the triangle.

3. Ask them to secure the foam sheet using the masking tape such that there are no sharp edges.
4. Next, ask the children to stick the coloured tapes over the masking tape.
5. Ensure that the children cover the eyepiece—through which they would peep into their kaleidoscope—as the sharp edges of the mirrors may hurt the children.
6. The kaleidoscopes are now ready for use!

How to Play:

1. Ask the children: If they placed a bead and looked through the Kaleidoscope, what would they see? Build curiosity during the conversation.
2. Next, keep only one bead in the dish and ask the children to peep through their kaleidoscopes, and ask them to count the number of images they are able to see.
3. Now, urge them to place two beads and ask them: How many images would they see now? Let them guess. Introduce math tables! Ask them to guess the images once again!
4. Then, ask them if they can find any connection between the number of beads and the images formed.

Tickle the Thoughts:

1. Ask the children what they see.
2. Ask them why they see so many beads.
3. Ask them how they think these images are formed.
4. What will happen if they made a square or a pentagonal kaleidoscope?

Goals Achieved

- Increased curiosity
- Improved concentration
- Better observation skills
- Enhanced numeracy skills

Tick-tack Tips

1. Do not give the answers to the child too quickly. Allow them to ponder over the questions.
2. Offer to make the kaleidoscope with more number of mirrors with the children.
3. Ask open-ended questions to build their curiosity further.

Activity–2

The Pipe Periscope!

RESOURCES REQUIRED

- 15- to 20-inches-long PVC pipe
- 2 curved elbow joints (to fit the PVC pipe)
- 2 circular flat mirrors (big enough to fit inside the PVC pipe)
- PVC adhesive
- Paint and a paintbrush

Getting Ready:

Keep one set of the required resources for each child.

Method:

1. Invite the children to take the pipe and fix the elbow joints on the opposite ends of the pipe such that the two openings face in opposite directions.
2. Now, ask them to place the circular mirrors where the pipe and the elbows meet and form a right angle. The two mirrors should be placed at a 45° angle inside the pipe, facing each other.

   TIP: In the periscope, light falls on the top mirror, which is placed at a 45° angle, it reflects and travels at the same angle.

3. Help the children adjust the two mirrors such that when the

light reflects from the first mirror and falls on the second mirror, it travels through the other opening for the child to see.

4. Place an object at one end of the periscope.
5. Encourage the children to adjust the mirrors until they can clearly see the object through the other opening of the periscope.
6. Once the image is clearly visible, help them fix the mirrors more firmly using the PVC adhesive.
7. Children can also paint the periscope.

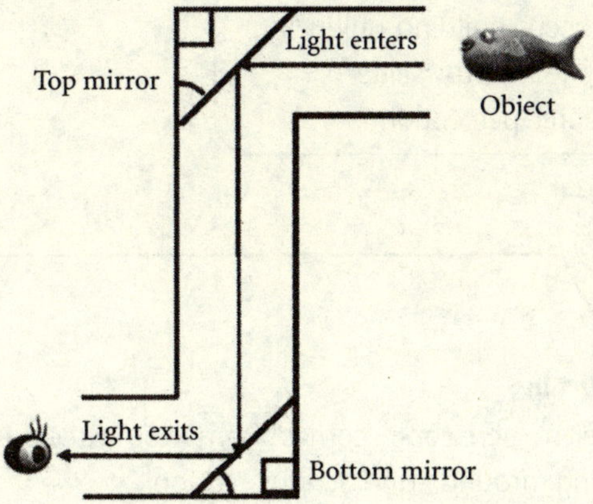

How Does It Work:

1. When you focus the top mirror on the object (fish) you want to see, the light reflects from the top mirror at the same angle that it falls on the bottom mirror. In the periscope, the light reflects from the top mirror at a 45° angle and falls on the mirror placed below it at the same angle. The light then moves out of the periscope and enters the eye of the child.

Tickle the Thoughts:

1. Ask the children what will happen if they use a longer or a shorter pipe.
2. Ask them what will happen if the surface of the mirror is rough, concave or convex.
3. Where can they use a periscope?
4. Ask them how they can see things more clearly.

Goals Achieved

- Enhanced curiosity
- Concept building abilities
- Refined motor skills
- Clearer perception

Tick-tack Tips

1. The term 'periscope' comes from two Greek words, *peri*, meaning 'around', and *scopus*, 'to look'.
2. A periscope is an instrument people use to look at things from a hidden position such as submarines. Submarines have periscopes so the sailors inside them can see what's on the surface of the water.
3. You can make your periscope longer, but longer the tube is, smaller will be the size of the image you'll see. Periscopes in tanks and submarines have magnifying lenses between the mirrors to make the reflection appear larger.

Activity–3

Floating Candles!

RESOURCES REQUIRED

- An old glass or a goblet
- 2 dozens of coloured pebbles
- Half a litre of water
- 100 ml of baby oil or refined cooking oil
- A few drops of food colour
- A wick
- A lighter

Getting Ready:

Keep goblets, coloured pebbles, water, wicks and a lighter (to light the floating candles) ready.

Method:

1. Invite the children to take the goblets, and place eight to ten pebbles inside it.
2. Pour water into the goblet and add a drop of food colour to it. Stir it well.
3. Add 30 to 40 ml of refined cooking oil into the goblet.
4. Now place the floating wick and help the children to light the candles.

Tickle the Thoughts:

1. Why are there two layers of liquids? What is the top layer made of—oil or water? Explain the concept of density of different kinds of liquids.
2. Ask the children if they stir the solution, will the oil get mixed with the water, or will the oil form a layer at the bottom of the vessel? Invite the children to give it a try!
3. Ask the children to stir the solution of water and oil; allow it to settle down while the children observe it. Then, ask them why has the oil not mixed with the water completely.
4. Why does oil form the top layer and water form the bottom layer?

Goals Achieved

- Increased curiosity
- Enhanced observation abilities
- Better concept building abilities
- Improved thinking skills

Tick-tack Tips

1. You can use different food colours for different occasions.
2. If baby oil is not available, then children may use other non-inflammable oils.
3. If pebbles are not available, then children may use artificial pearls.
4. Don't forget to add food colour drop by drop to get the desired shade of the solution, as the artificial pearls will not be visible

in very dark solutions.

5. To further their interests in the density of liquids, pour 5 ml of each of the below-mentioned liquids into a glass:

   - Honey
   - Sugar syrup
   - Dishwashing liquid
   - Water
   - Edible oil

   In the glass, honey will form the last layer; the sugar syrup will form the next layer; then, the dishwashing liquid will form the next one; water comes next; and finally, edible oil will form the first layer. These layers will form a beautiful set of different colours.

Activity–4

Trick-O-Treat Boxes!

RESOURCES REQUIRED

- Empty carton or cardboard gift boxes
- An old doll
- 250 g of vaseline petroleum jelly
- 1 roll of gauze cloth
- Starch spray
- Acrylic paints
- Paintbrushes
- A pair of child-safe scissors

Getting Ready:

1. Keep a set of the required resources for each child.
2. Cut gauze into ten to fifteen large pieces, enough to cover the doll's head.

Method:

1. Invite the children to apply vaseline liberally all over the doll's head.
2. Next, ask the children to place the gauze on the doll's head. Tell them to gently press it with their fingers so that the gauze takes the shape of the doll's head. Then, spray starch all over it.
3. Apply a few more layers of gauzes and spray starch after

each layer. Repeat it till there is a thick layer of gauze on the doll's head. Allow it to dry.

4. Now, gently remove the dry layer from the doll's head.
5. Stick the dried gauze, which is in the shape of the doll's head, on the carton and use acrylic paint to give it a scary look. Allow the paint to dry overnight.
6. Place Halloween treats inside the box. The box is now ready to scare your children's friends.

Tickle the Thoughts:

1. Ask the children what is fear.
2. What do they fear the most?
3. Whom do they want to scare?
4. How would they make scarier boxes?

Goals Achieved

- Enhanced curiosity
- Better concept-building abilities
- Increased thinking skills
- Improved association techniques

Tick-tack Tip

You can also make photo frames or even hang scary dolls using the same technique!

Activity–5

The Prop's Up!

RESOURCES REQUIRED

- A few props such as pencil box, a book, a stone or a brick, twigs, broom, etc.
- A tray
- A napkin to cover the tray

Getting Ready:

Keep the props on the tray covered with a napkin so that children do not get to cheat! Keep the curiosity alive during the activity.

How to Play:

1. Ask the children to sit in a circle.
2. Assign a number to each child.
3. Invite a child to begin the game by pulling out a prop from under the napkin and showing it to the other children.
4. The child will then ask the player sitting next to him or her in the circle to imagine five different uses of the given prop.
5. The idea is to encourage the imagination of children and not pressurize them to get the maximum score. However, if you are keeping scores, count the number of uses given by each child at the end of the game. Assign a child to count the total score. The child with the maximum score wins the game!

For example:

1. If the first player pulls out a stone from the tray and another child is asked to list five different uses of that prop, the second child may come up with the following answers:

   - As a door stopper
   - As a paper weight
   - To stop a rolling wheel of a car or cycle
   - Used for decorational purposes
   - To throw it into the water to create ripples

Tickle the Thoughts:

1. If the properties of the prop are changed, for example, if the stone is broken into smaller pieces, ask the children how will they use the prop.
2. What are pebbles made of?
3. Where can one find stones?
4. Are there stones on the moon as well?

Goals Achieved

- Enhanced curiosity
- Better association techniques
- Increased visualization abilities
- Improved perception

Tick-tack Tips

1. Help the children to think by changing the properties of the prop, such as the location and time. This will encourage the child to think of different ideas.
2. Increase the number of props to stretch the game for a longer span of time.

Activity–6

Glow-in-the-Dark Play Dough!

RESOURCES REQUIRED

- A mixing bowl and a spoon
- A measuring scale
- 1 cup of flour
- 1/2 cup of salt
- 2 tablespoons of cream of tartar
- 1 tablespoon of vegetable oil
- 1 cup of boiling water
- 2 tablespoons of glow-in-the-dark paint

Getting Ready:

Keep one set of the required resources for each child.

Method:

1. Invite the children to measure the ingredients using the measuring scale.
2. Help them add the measured flour, salt, cream of tartar and vegetable oil to the mixing bowl, and blend everything together.
3. Help the children add a little boiling water as they blend the ingredients.
4. Add some more water until it gets fully incorporated.
5. Add glow-in-the-dark paint and once again blend it well.

6. The glow-in-the-dark play dough is ready for use!

How to Play:

1. Switch off all the lights in the room and ensure that there is complete darkness.
2. Watch the play dough glow. Make various spooky shapes to scare friends in the dark!

Tickle the Thoughts:

1. Ask the children to explain light.
2. Ask them what happens when the lights in a room are switched on.
3. Ask them if the play dough glows in the dark.

Goals Achieved

- Increased curiosity
- Enhanced association abilities
- Clearer perception
- Improved sensory skills

Tick-tack Tip

If the glow-in-the-dark paint is not available, you can add food colour or glitter and use the mixture as coloured play dough.

Activity–7

Lava Lamps!

RESOURCES REQUIRED

- Food colour
- A dropper for each child
- A drinking glass
- 1/4th glass of water for each child
- 1/2 glass of vegetable oil for each child
- Fizz tablets

Getting Ready:

Keep one set of the required resources for each child.

Method:

1. Invite the children to add two drops of food colour into their respective glasses using a dropper.
2. Urge them to fill quarter of the glass with water.
3. Ask them to add two quarters of vegetable oil to the glass, i.e., twice the amount of water.
4. Leave one quarter of the glass empty to prevent the fizz from spilling over.
5. Ask the children to drop a fizz tablet into their respective glasses.

Tickle the Thoughts:

1. Now, ask the children what would happen after they dropped their fizz tablets into their respective glasses. Will the fizz tablet merely melt into the glass, or will it explode, or will it create a spooky effect to scare their friends at night?
2. Why did they need to add water?
3. Why are there bubbles in the solution?

Goals Achieved

- Enhanced curiosity
- Increased association techniques
- Improved sensory skills

Tick-tack Tips

1. Fix a light source from under the glass for better results.
2. For a spooky effect, children may use different food colours.

Activity–8

Scratch for Surprise!

RESOURCES REQUIRED

- A mixing bowl
- Two teaspoons of acrylic paint
- Two teaspoons of dishwashing soap
- A contact sheet
- An A4-sized sheet
- A pair of child-safe scissors
- 1 coin

Getting Ready:

Keep all the required resources ready.

Method:

1. Tell the children to pour the acrylic paint into a bowl and add the dishwashing soap to it in the required proportions.
2. Ask them to mix it well and keep it aside.
3. Then, ask the children to take a contact paper and apply the prepared solution on its non-sticky side. Let it dry.
4. Next, ask the children to write the secret message on an A4-sized sheet.
5. Tell them to cut the contact paper large enough to cover the secret message.
6. Ask them to remove the thin film of paper on the reverse

side of contact paper and stick this contact paper over the secret message. The secret message is ready.

7. Hand over a coin to another child and request him or her to scratch the surface to read the secret surprise.

Tickle the Thoughts:

1. Ask the children what are secrets.
2. Why do they need to hide the secret messages?
3. How else they can write secret messages?
4. Where else they can write a surprise message for a friend?
5. Why was the dish soap added to the acrylic paint?

Goals Achieved

- Enhanced curiosity
- Increased association abilities
- Improved sensory skills

Tick-tack Tips

1. Make greeting cards with secret messages for the reader.
2. Mark various continents and countries on the map for children to scratch and discover!
3. Inform children about the ancient methods of writing and sending secret messages such as Morse Codes.
4. To add some fun to the 'secrets', tell them that in ancient days people were made to shave off their hair, a secret message was tattooed on the messenger's head and was sent to the receiver of the message after his hair had grown again!

5. In the remote mountains of northern Turkey, the villagers use a sophisticated, highly-developed and high-pitched form of whistling to communicate amongst the villagers. This language is called 'bird language'. The UNESCO has declared it as an endangered part of world heritage as only 10,000 people know this language, and it needs to be protected. It is now being taught in schools, and the villagers now have an annual festival to celebrate 'bird language'.

Activity–9

Mush-gill Prints!

RESOURCES REQUIRED

- 1 button mushroom per child
- 4–5 poster colours
- 1 chart paper
- 2 bowls
- 4 toothbrushes
- A pair of child-safe scissors

Getting Ready:

Cut the chart paper into A4-sized sheets and keep them ready for use.

Method:

1. Invite the children to take the pre-cut chart papers and place them on the table.
2. Ask them to pour one of the poster colours, of their choice, into their bowls.
3. Ask them to dip the caps of the button mushrooms into the paint and press them gently on the chart paper. The mushrooms will leave imprints on the paper.
4. Cover the mushrooms' caps with clean bowls and leave them to dry overnight.
5. Before removing the bowls the next day, ask the children to

take a toothbrush, dip it in a poster colour of their choice and, using their thumbs, spray them around the bowls.

6. Once the spray print has dried, ask the children to uncover the mushrooms to discover the unusual prints the mushroom's gills have imprinted.

Tickle the Thoughts:

1. Ask the children what patterns they would see on uncovering their paintings.
2. Which aquatic animal has gills?
3. Do plants have gills? Do plants breathe through gills too?

Goals Achieved

- Enhanced curiosity
- Clearer perception
- Improved sensory skills

Tick-tack Tip

Children may use different types of mushrooms, such as oyster mushrooms, to make different kinds of prints.

Activity–10

Flour Batik!

RESOURCES REQUIRED

- 1 cotton t-shirt per child
- 500 g of flour
- 1 litre of cold water
- 1 plastic sheet
- 1 paintbrush (thin)
- Batik dye
- 1 pair of hand gloves
- A mixing bowl

Getting Ready:

Cover the surface the children will be working on with newspapers.

Method:

1. Invite the children to place the t-shirts on the table. Ask them to place plastic sheets inside the t-shirt—the front and back—to prevent the dye from bleeding into any other part.
2. Ask them to mix flour and water in a mixing bowl and then add water little by little to get a thin paste without lumps.
3. Help the children to mix the dye and water as per the instructions given on the packet.
4. Next, urge them to dip their paintbrushes into the flour-water paste and paint a design on their respective t-shirts. Allow

the paste to dry over-night.

5. As the children brush the dye on their respective t-shirts, ask them what would happen if they brushed the dye onto the designs made? Give them time to think and respond.
6. Then, fill a bucket of cold water to rinse the t-shirts. Use fresh cold water to rinse each t-shirt. Hang the t-shirts to dry overnight.
7. Help the children to iron the t-shirts gently to secure the colours.

Tickle the Thoughts:

1. Explain to them how the art of flour batik has evolved over the centuries.
2. What other materials can be used instead of flour and water paste?
3. Where else can batik paints be used?

Goals Achieved

- Enhanced curiosity
- Improved visualization abilities
- Enhanced sensory skills

Tick-tack Tips

1. Children may experiment by adding borders on the sleeves of the t-shirts as well.
2. The t-shirts make great birthday party gifts, as children can make designs specific to the occasion.

Activity–11

Tie and Dye!

RESOURCES REQUIRED

- 1 pair of rubber gloves
- 1 apron
- Plain cotton scarves or stoles
- 1 lead pencil
- 1 pack of rubber bands
- Cold water dye
- A broad-based bucket
- Marbles and beads of different sizes
- 1 iron

Getting Ready:

1. Cover the work surface to protect it from dye stains.
2. Ask the children to wear gloves and aprons as the dye might stain their hands and clothes.

Method:

1. Help the children draw a design using the lead pencils on their scarves.
2. Now, ask them to tie the beads on the lines using rubber bands.
3. Next, ask them to use the rubber bands to tie marbles and beads from one side of the scarf over the design.

4. Ask them to tie another rubber band underneath the first one, leaving some part of the scarf exposed to absorb the colour.
5. Help the children to read the instructions given on the packet of the dye.
6. Ask them to fill the bucket with adequate quantity of water and add the dye as per the instructions given.
7. Now, ask the children to submerge the scarf into the dye as per the instructions given on the packet of dye. Leave it submerged for five minutes.
8. Remove the scarves and dry them in the shade along with the marbles and the beads.
9. The next day, before the children remove the marbles, build their curiosity by asking them to guess what would have happened to the scarves and the marbles. Then, encourage them to remove the rubber bands and the marbles. Keep up the element of surprise!
10. Soak the scarves in cold water until no more colour bleeds. Allow them to dry.
11. Set the iron on low heat and encourage the children to iron the scarves. Make sure there is an adult supervising them, as they use the hot iron.

Tickle the Thoughts:

1. Ask the children how the patterns were formed.
2. Why did the colour not spread to places where the rubber bands were tied?
3. Where else can they use the tie and dye technique?
4. How can they make different patterns?

Goals Achieved

- Enhanced curiosity
- Improved visualization
- Refined fine motor skills
- Better sensory skills

Tick-tack Tips

1. Tie and dye bedsheets and saris make good gifts.
2. Children enjoy making psychedelic designs on cotton socks!

Activity–12

Bird Piñatas!

RESOURCES REQUIRED

- 2 balloons
- 1 can of PVA glue
- A pair of child-safe scissors
- 1 bottle of spray paint
- 1 packet of mixed candies as novelties
- 1 wooden stick
- A scarf to blindfold the children
- A bed sheet

Getting Ready:

Explain to the children that piñatas are party decorations that have candies hidden inside. To get these candies, the children need to knock down the piñatas with a stick while they are blindfolded. The candies then fall on the ground and the children rush to pick them up.

Method:

1. Ask the children to inflate two balloons and secure its ends so that the air does not escape. One balloon should be bigger than the other.
2. Ask them to tear up a newspaper into small bits and stick them using the glue on both the balloons.

3. Ask the children to repeat these steps until they get four to five layers of well-pasted paper on both the balloons. Ensure that no part of the balloon is left exposed.
4. Let the balloons dry.
5. After the newspaper bits on the balloons have dried up, cut open a hole into the balloons for the neck for the bird and keep the cutout to be used later. Do not worry if the balloon bursts during this process. By now, the dry newspaper bits would have become strong enough to retain the shape, without the balloon.
6. Ask the children to paint the piñatas once again and let them dry.
7. Ask them to take the cardboard roll inside the toilet paper roll and insert it in the cutout hole to make the neck of the bird and fix the second smaller-sized balloon on the other side of the toilet paper roll to make the head of the piñata.
8. Using crepe paper, make a cone for the beak of the bird. Stick googly eyes, use streamers to make wings and make the claws by sticking toilet paper rolls and painting them with dark colours. Fill up the bird piñatas with candies before sealing the opening.
9. Now, hand over a few streamers to children to make the tail of the bird.

   TIP: Spread a sheet under the piñata so that when the candies fall on the ground, they do not get dirty.

10. Once again, paint the piñata to give finishing touches to the bird.
11. Now, fix a hook on the piñata such that it balances well when hung from the roof.
12. Then, blindfold a child and allow only three attempts per child to break the piñata.

13. Before the child makes the first attempt, push the piñata so that it swings, making it difficult for him or her to break it.

Tickle the Thoughts:

1. Ask them if they want to break the bird piñata.
2. How else can they use the bird piñata?

Goals Achieved

- Increased curiosity
- Improved attention
- Enhanced observation skills
- Ablity to follow multiple-step instructions

Tick-tack Tips

1. Children can fix the knotted balloon on a water bottle's cap to prevent it from flying away, while they are working on it.
2. Bird piñata can also be used as money bank for children to save money.

Activity–13

Astronaut's Adventure!

RESOURCES REQUIRED

- 1 large carton
- 1 child-safe knife
- A pair of child-safe scissors
- Crepe paper according to the different colours of planets (refer to Tick-tack Tips)
- Paint and paintbrushes
- Old science magazines
- Glue
- An old bedsheet

Getting Ready:

Keep the required resources ready before the adventure begins on earth!

Method:

1. Invite the children to take a large carton, say a rectangular T.V. carton, and cut it into half using the child-safe knife or scissors.
2. Now, ask the children to paint the carton black from inside to represent space. Once the paint has dried up, ask the children to take the old magazines and cut out pictures of the things relevant to space, such as pictures of spaceships,

astronauts and space stations. Stick them on or hang them from the top of the carton.

3. Ask the children to take the coloured crepe paper and crush them into balls of different sizes. Help them match the colours of crepe paper to those of the planets.
4. Tie a thread around each planet made of paper. Leave one end of the thread long enough to be tied to the ceiling of the carton.
5. Ask them to drill small holes into the carton and hang the planets using the long end of the thread.
6. Then, ask the children to place the biggest yellow ball—the sun—also made of crushed paper, on one end, either right or left, of the carton. Hang the remaining planets in the carton in the ascending order of the distance of the planets from the sun.
7. Lastly, ask them to cover the roof of the carton with chart paper to hide the knots of threads, giving the carton a neat look.

Tickle the Thoughts:

1. Take the children out at night and spread a sheet under the star-lit sky. Ask them to lie down next to you on the sheet and tell you what they see in the sky.
2. Help them spot stars, planets and constellations.
3. Where is outer space?
4. How do people travel to space?
5. Explain the concept of space stations. How do they work? What kind of work do astronauts do?

Goals Achieved

- Enhanced curiosity
- Improved attention
- Better association abilities
- Clearer perception

Tick-tack Tips

The colours of the planets mentioned below may vary slightly. For example, Jupiter reflects different shades of white, red, orange, brown and yellow. The colours of Jupiter's atmosphere are created when different chemicals reflect the light from the sun. Changes in the colour of the planet are affected by storms and winds in its atmosphere.

- Sun (star) – Yellow
- Planets – Colour of planets
- Mercury – Gray
- Venus – Pale yellow
- Earth – Blue and green
- Mars – Reddish brown
- Jupiter – Orange
- Saturn – Pale gold
- Uranus – Pale blue-green
- Neptune – Pale blue

Activity–14

Scary Scarecrow!

RESOURCES REQUIRED

- A newspaper
- A pair of child-safe scissors
- 2 bamboo garden stakes
- Straw or hay
- 2 shopping bags
- 5 metres of jute rope
- A piece of square hessian cloth–40 cm
- A black marking pen
- 1 table tennis ball
- A PVA glue can
- Old clothes–hat, shirt, scarf, jeans and gloves
- A wooden board

Getting Ready:

To avoid wastage, first help the children with cutting a tissue paper into a circle before cutting the hessian cloth.

How to Cut a Circle:

1. Encourage children to take a square tissue paper, fold it in half. Fold it into another half to resemble an ice-cream cone.
2. Ask the children to fix a pencil into the compass and place the pointed end of the compass at the closed end of the

tissue paper and draw an arc.

3. With the child-safe scissors, ask them to cut along the arc. Open it into a full circle.
4. Make the children practise cutting a few more tissue papers before they cut the hessian cloth.

Making the Head of the Scary Scarecrow:

1. Ask the children to cut the hessian cloth into a circle using the above-mentioned process.
2. Next, ask them to take a shopping bag and fill it up with straw. Place it at the centre of the circular hessian cloth. Fix the bamboo stake vertically inside the shopping bag. Bring all the edges of the circular hessian cloth together such that it forms a *potli*, a small round-bottomed bag. Secure the bamboo with a jute rope.
3. Help the children to cut the table tennis balls into halves for the eyes of the scarecrow and place them on the head. Draw a black circle on the convex side of the tennis balls. Once they are done with the eyes, cutout felt pieces to make eyebrows, a moustache and a mouth, and stick them on the face with the help of PVA glue.

Making the Body of the Scarecrow:

1. Ask the children to fill up the shopping bag with straw. Pass the second bamboo stake through the loops of the shopping bag, and fix the two stake such that they intersect each other at their centres. This makes the hands of the scarecrow. Put on the shirt for the scarecrow now.
2. Stuff the sleeves with straw. Leave some straw sticking out of the sleeves to make the hands look scary. Secure the ends of the sleeves by tying them up with jute ropes.
3. Stuff the jeans with straws and secure the end of the legs

with jute ropes. Leave the straw sticking out at the end.

4. Attach the upper half of the body to the lower half by passing another jute rope through the loops of the jeans. Secure the bamboo at the same time.
5. Tie a scarf around the neck of the scarecrow to finish.

Tickle the Thoughts:

1. Ask the children why it is called a scarecrow.
2. Why does it need to be scary?
3. Do the birds really get scared?
4. What scares them the most?

Goals Achieved

- Increased curiosity
- Improved observation skills
- Enhanced association abilities
- Clearer perception
- Enhanced ability to process multiple-step instructions

Tick-tack Tips

1. Everybody is scared of something or the other, but one must understand that 'fear is a milestone'.
2. This activity is a good opportunity for the parents to find the hidden fears and reservations of their child. Go easy on the child during the activity.
3. Asking open-ended questions will be the master key to unlock your child's hidden fears. Happy unlocking!

Activity–15

Spooky Edible Brain Specimen!

RESOURCES REQUIRED

- 1 watermelon
- 1 big glass bowl
- 1 litre of thick blueberry juice
- 1 clean paintbrush
- 2 litres of apple juice

Getting Ready:

1. Keep the juices ready.
2. Peel the green and white cover of the watermelon and split it into two halves.
3. The blueberry juice should have a thick consistency.

Method:

1. Ask the children to dip a clean paintbrush into the blueberry juice and begin to draw the lines on the convex side of the watermelon resembling the wrinkles of the brain.
2. Next, help them to gently carve 1 cm-deep wrinkles on the watermelon and place it into a big glass bowl filled with apple juice.
3. The spooky edible brain specimen is ready for the young scientists to study.

Tickle the Thoughts:

1. Encourage the children to role-play scientists and give them adequate time to talk about their observations regarding various organs.
2. Ask the children about the different organs.
3. Why do scientists need to keep the specimens in solutions?

Goals Achieved

- Increased curiosity
- Improved communication skills
- Better observation abilities
- Enhanced association skills

Tick-tack Tips

1. For spooky effects, place the jar in a dark room and switch on a bulb behind the jar.
2. Children may create a model of the brain using noodles, by boiling them in coloured water. They can use different colours for the various parts of the brain.

Attention

Activity–16

The Battle of Balloon Grenades!

RESOURCES REQUIRED

- Skin-friendly colours for painting the face
- 2 paintbrushes
- 25 to 30 small balloons per team
- Water
- 1 water gun
- 1 plastic tray per team member
- Change of clothes

Getting Ready:

1. Ask the children to paint their teammate's face into that of a warrior's.
2. Draw two lines on the ground for the two teams to stand apart.

How to Play:

1. Ask children to form two teams and ask the teams to stand at the lines marked. Allocate numbers to each team such as Team 1 and Team 2.
2. Ask Team 1 to take the water gun, fill their set of balloons with water and tie knots to secure the ends.
3. Give each member of Team 2 a tray to block the balloon grenades shot by their opponent.

4. Set the timer to two minutes and count the number of balloon grenades that hit the warriors of the opponent team!
5. Each team gets their turn to throw and block the grenades.
6. At the end of the game, count the number of successful targets achieved by both the teams. The team with most hits is the winner.

Goals Achieved

- Improved attention span
- Building teamwork
- Enhanced gross motor skills

Tick-tack Tips

1. Have the children play this game outdoors as the water from the balloon grenades will spill and children might slip on the smooth surface.
2. You can also use warrior masks or grease to give a more suitable effect to the children!

Activity–17

Beach Treasures!

RESOURCES REQUIRED

- 1 piece of driftwood
- 20 to 25 shells
- 15 to 18 pebbles
- 3-metre-long rope
- 5-metres-long string
- 15 to 20 wooden beads

Getting Ready:

Keep some extra time to go to the seashore, with the children, to collect shells, pebbles, driftwoods and other natural products that are available in the surroundings to create art and lasting souvenirs!

Method:

1. Once back home, ask the children to use a string to hang all the things from the driftwood. Parents may help them tie the things onto the driftwood.
2. Then, ask them to take the rope and tie it on both the sides of the driftwood to make a wall hanging.

Tickle the Thoughts:

1. Ask the children how they want to decorate the driftwood.
2. What else do they think could be added to it?
3. Would they like to string their picture with the beads?

Goals Achieved

- Improved attention span
- Refined fine motor skills
- Freedom of choice

Tick-tack Tips

1. Hang the unique things at the bottom of the string.
2. If wrapping the string around some pieces is difficult for the child, then drill a small hole into the pebbles and shells.

Activity–18

Paper Weave for Book Covers!

RESOURCES REQUIRED

- Card papers
- Textured greeting cards
- 1 child-safe craft knife
- 1 pair of child-safe scissors
- 1 glue
- 1 cutting board
- 1 scale
- 1 lead pencil

Getting Ready:

Save the greeting cards that have textured papers, for recycling and making beautiful book covers.

Method:

1. Invite the children to choose the textured cards for their book's cover.
2. Ask them to measure the dimensions of the book and cut the card paper slightly bigger than the actual size of the book.
3. Ask the children to place the card on the cutting board. Urge them to use the scale to draw horizontal lines on the reverse side of the card paper, leaving 1 cm margin on both sides, so that the lines are not visible later.

4. Under your supervision, ask them to carefully run the child-safe craft knife on the marked lines and make slits in the card. Ensure not to cut all the way to the sides of the craft paper.
5. Now, ask the children to use the child-safe scissors to cut strips of old recyclable textured greeting cards.
6. Then, urge them to weave the paper strips such that the vertical strip goes over the first horizontal strip and under the next horizontal strip.
7. Lastly, glue the ends of the strips and paste this on the book.

Tickle the Thoughts:

1. Ask the children to go around the house and get whatever they think is woven.
2. How can they create more weaving patterns?
3. What other materials would they like to use for weaving?

Goals Achieved

- Improved attention span
- Refined fine motor skills
- Enhanced sense of achievement

Tick-tack Tips

1. Children can make zigzag slits or even diagonal curves on the card paper.
2. To make weaving patterns, children can alternate each row to create a professional look!

Activity–19

Bamboo Chimes!

RESOURCES REQUIRED

- 1 wooden embroidery hoop
- 2 to 4 bamboos per hoop
- 12 to 25 shells
- 10 to 12 feathers
- 3-metre-long ropes
- 5-metre-long strings
- 15 to 20 wooden beads
- 2 to 3 pictures of children

Getting Ready:

Keep the required resources ready for each child.

Method:

1. Invite the children to take three to four strings to tie shells, pebbles, beads, feathers and their pictures onto them.
2. Ask them to knot the strings to the wooden embroidery hoop at equal distances.
3. Next, ask the children to tie the bamboos to the hoop. Ensure that the bamboos are well spaced so that the hoop remains balanced.
4. Lastly, encourage the children to hang the bamboo chimes in the balcony or from a window such that the breeze moves the bamboos and makes pleasant sounds.

Tickle the Thoughts:

1. Ask the children what else could be added to a wind chime.
2. What is sound?
3. Where does the sound go after they have heard it?
4. Does the sound also travel in cars as they do? How does it travel from you to them?
5. Can fishes in water also hear sounds?

Goals Achieved

- Improved attention span
- Enhanced sensory skills
- Helps to understand 'reduce the waste' and 'recycle the resources'

Tick-tack Tip

To wrap the string around some pieces might be a little difficult; you may drill small holes into the bamboos.

Activity–20

Fun with Bags!

RESOURCES REQUIRED

- Bags of different kinds
- Wooden beads
- 5-metre-long laces
- 1 pair of child-safe scissors
- 3 to 4 craft pens
- 1 PVA glue
- Sewing needle and threads matching the colour of the bags
- 1 pencil

Getting Ready:

1. Save the bags that you thought you would throw away for a new classy one.
2. Keep a few easy designs for the children to begin their work with.

Method:

1. Invite the children to choose a bag to work on.

   Woven bags:

   i. Ask them to draw a design on the bag using a pencil.

   ii. With the sewing needle, help the children sew the beads along the design.

Plain plastic beach bags:

i. Ask the children to use craft pens to draw designs. Encourage them to focus on the designs, as smudging will make the bags look untidy.

Tickle the Thoughts:

1. How were bags invented?
2. Ask the children what they think the first bag looked like. Can they draw it?
3. What are the things that need to be in the bag all the time?

Goals Achieved

- Increased attention span
- Refined fine motor skills
- Enhanced organization skills
- Improved association abilities

Tick-tack Tips

1. This activity gives parents the opportunity to inculcate organizing skills in the children. Encourage them to organize their belongings in their school bags.
2. Children look smart if they match their hats and bags for a birthday party.
3. Artificial flowers can be added to the bags to make them look trendy.

Activity–21

Place Mats!

RESOURCES REQUIRED

- 2 white chart papers
- 1 pair of child-safe scissors
- 1 cereal box
- 1 poster colour box
- 6 marbles
- 6 mixing bowls
- 1 clear contact sheet
- 1 ruler

Getting Ready:

1. Save empty cereal boxes for later use.

Method:

1. Invite the children to use the child-safe scissors to cut open the recyclable cereal box such that it gets a base large enough to fit the chart paper. Ask them to cut and fix the paper into the carton's inner base.
2. Ask them to pour poster colours into mixing bowls and put some marbles in each bowl.
3. Now, encourage the children to decide and choose a colour of their choice. Using a teaspoon, ask them to pick a marble at a time and make the marbles roll on the chart paper by tilting the box back and forth.

4. Children don't need to wait for the paint trail made by a marble to dry up before rolling the next one. Allow them the time to explore the possibilities and observe the crossover of the trails that the marbles make on the paper.
5. Allow the painting to dry.
6. Ask the children to now take two sheets of clear contact paper that are about 2.5 cm longer and wider than the painting.
7. Ask the children to sandwich the painting between the two layers of the clear contact papers and press the surface of the sheets using a scale such that all the air bubbles are removed.
8. The place mats are ready to be placed on the tables!

Tickle the Thoughts:

1. What are primary colours?
2. Ask the children to guess which new colour will be made if the blue marble's trail gets mixed with yellow.
3. What are secondary and tertiary colours?

Goals Achieved

- Better attention span
- Improved decision-making skills
- Seeks and explores possibilities
- Enhanced sensory skills

Tick-tack Tip

For a more professional look, children can get the painting laminated! The laminate is easy to keep clean.

Activity–22

Feed the Santa!

RESOURCES REQUIRED

- 1 large carton
- 1 quarter plate
- 1 black marker
- Poster colours
- 2 broad paintbrushes
- Thin paintbrushes
- 1 cotton roll
- 1 glue
- 1 small soft rubber ball
- Aprons for each child

Getting Ready:

1. Ask the children to wear their aprons.
2. Cover the work surface with newspapers.

Method:

1. Invite the children to take the empty carton and place a quarter plate on it. Using the black marker, ask them to draw a circle around the plate.
2. Next, ask them to cut a hole along the marked line to form Santa's mouth. Ensure that the hole is large enough for a small soft rubber ball to pass through it.

3. Using the broad brushes, paint the carton light brown to make Santa's face. Next, paint his eyes white and mark his eyeballs with the black marker.
4. Apply glue on the carton to paste Santa's beard and moustache. Stick the cotton to make his moustache and beard!
5. Paint his cap red and the ball at its tip with white.

How to Play:

1. Ask each child to take a soft rubber ball and line up in front of Santa.
2. Now, ask them to throw the ball into Santa's mouth one at a time. To feed Santa, the ball has to pass through his mouth.

Tickle the Thoughts:

1. Is Santa real?
2. Where do they think Santa lives and what does he eat?

Goals Achieved

- Improved attention span
- Enhanced gross motor skills
- Refined fine motor skills
- Encourages imagination

Tick-tack Tips

1. Using the same method, children may make a clown instead of a Santa.
2. To keep the carton from falling over, put a few heavy objects inside it.

Activity–23

Fairy Terrariums!

RESOURCES REQUIRED

- 1 broad-based glass jar
- 1 kg of pebbles/gravel
- 500 g of soil
- 100 g of activated charcoal
- Moss
- A spoon and a fork
- Toys such as fairies, magic wands, castles, wishing wells, etc.
- Plants such as succulents

Getting Ready:

Save the big broad glass jars to make a low-maintenance mini-garden for the children's study table.

Method:

1. Invite the children to take one glass jar each and add a layer of pebbles.
2. Next, ask them to pour activated charcoal into it, and then pour a thick layer of soil.
3. Ask the children to place a layer of moss that will hold the moisture for the plants.
4. Now, encourage them to place the toys to create a fairyland.

5. Ask the children to find a spot to keep the terrarium in their room.
6. Encourage them to sprinkle water occasionally in the terrarium.

Tickle the Thoughts:

1. What is an ecosystem?
2. What is the purpose of putting a layer of pebbles first?
3. What is activated charcoal and what does it do?
4. How are plants and animals interdependent on each other for survival?

Goals Achieved

- Enhanced attention span
- Encourages fantasies and imagination
- Better concept-building abilities

Tick-tack Tips

1. Talk to the children about fairies. It is a good opportunity to dig into the thoughts of a child and find their hidden desires and fears. Ask open-ended questions.
2. Instead of trying to reach the corners of a rectangular glass jar with your fingers, use rubber bands to tie a pair of chopsticks to reach the corners.
3. Study table is a good place to keep the terrarium.
4. Depending upon your geographical location, you may ask your local plant nursery about the best plants suitable for your child's room.

Activity–24

Salt-dough Curtains!

RESOURCES REQUIRED

For Salt-dough:
- 4 portions of flour
- 1 portion of salt
- 1 portion of cold water
- 3 to 4 food colours
- A box of toothpicks

For Curtains:
- Beads
- Cords or strings
- 1 nail paint
- 1 measuring tape

Getting Ready:

1. Keep the salt-dough ready before the children begin to make the curtains.

Method to Make Salt-dough:

1. Ask the children to take all the required resources in the proportions as mentioned and help them knead them into a soft dough.
2. Ask the children to divide the dough into four portions and add a few drops of food colour to each of them. Help the

children to knead them separately.
3. Next, ask them to roll out the salt-dough and make small balls.
4. Now, ask them to take the balls. Pass a toothpick through the centre of each ball to make a hole for the string to pass through later. Do not take out the toothpicks.
5. Allow the balls to dry. The salt-dough balls are now the ready 'beads' that are required to make into curtains!

Method to Make the Curtains:

1. Now that the beads are dry and ready, ask the children to remove the toothpicks carefully.
2. Next, ask the children to take a drop of nail paint and apply it at the end of the cord. Tell them to pinch it between the fingers such that, on drying, its end is pointed and it is easy for the children to thread the beads.
3. Encourage the children to measure the length of the window or the door, where they wish to hang the cords of beads to make it into a curtain.
4. Now, ask the children to cut the cord 4 inches longer than the length of the window so that they don't fall short of the required length when 'knotting the cord'.
5. Then, ask them to begin threading the beads.
6. Help them to knot the beads at the end of each cord to keep the beads from slipping out.
7. Finally, help the children hang the cords.

Tickle the Thoughts:

1. Ask them why we need curtains.
2. What is privacy?
3. Why is privacy important?

Goals Achieved

- Understanding the concept of privacy
- Introduction to 'good touch' and 'bad touch'
- Goal-driven
- Encourages persistence
- Encourages attention span
- Exercised fine motor skills

Tick-tack Tips

1. Ensure that there is a curtain rod fitted prior to the activity.
2. Guide the conversation towards 'privacy' by asking open-ended questions.
3. Young children need to understand the importance of privacy, and this activity gives parents an opportunity to understand the child's requirements.
4. A lot of schools are making conscious efforts to ensure the safety and security of children by introducing 'good touch' and 'bad touch'. However, parents need to help their child further. Parents can assess the surroundings at home and explain the concept in a different setting other than the school's surroundings. Make sure that you make the child aware of the dangers with a positive approach, and also confident enough to face the danger rather than scaring the child.

Activity–25

Fridge Magnets!

RESOURCES REQUIRED

For Salt-dough:

- 4 portions of flour
- 1 portion of salt
- 1 portion of cold water
- Cookie cutters of different shapes

For Fridge Magnets:

- Salt-dough
- 6 magnets
- Poster colours
- Paintbrushes

Getting Ready:

1. Keep salt-dough ready before the children begin to make their fridge magnets.
2. Keep a number of objects for testing the magnets.

Method:

1. Invite the children to knead the required resources in their right proportions into soft dough.
2. Ask the children to divide the dough according to the number of children.
3. Tell them to roll out their respective doughs.

4. Next, ask them to use the cookie cutters carefully to make different shapes. Ask the children to gently press the dough onto the magnets, and allow them to dry.
5. Now, ask the children to paint the fridge magnets with the poster colours. Let the paint dry.

TIP: Allow the children the time to experiment sticking the magnets onto various things available at home. Encourage them to experiment and form their own hypothesis.

Tickle the Thoughts:

1. What are magnets?
2. Why do some things stick to the magnets and some don't and others repel?

Goals Achieved

- Improved attention span
- Enhanced observation
- Better reasoning skills
- Form their own hypothesis

Tick-tack Tip

Show the children that by rubbing iron on a magnet, the iron turns into a temporary magnet. Call them 'copycat magnets'!

Activity–26

Mosaic Cushions!

RESOURCES REQUIRED:

- Old plain cushion covers
- Embroidery hoops for each cushion
- 1 pencil
- Vegetables: 1 carrot, 10 ladies fingers
- 1 child-safe knife
- 1 plastic sheet
- Fabric colours as per the design
- 2 sheets of tracing paper
- 1 iron

Getting Ready:

1. Assist the children to neatly cut different shapes of vegetables such as ladies fingers or carrots to use as stamps.

Method:

1. Invite the children to fix the cushion cover on the hoop tightly. Using a pencil, assist them to draw a design of their choice on the cushion cover.
2. Place a plastic sheet between the top and the bottom layers of the cover to keep the colour from seeping through the layers.
3. Next, ask the children to dip the vegetables in different fabric

colours and begin stamping on the covers to make more designs.

4. Allow the mosaic print to dry. Place a sheet of tracing paper on it and iron lightly to make the prints permanent.
5. Remove the tracing paper, and the cushion covers are ready for display!

Tickle the Thoughts:

1. Ask the children what other objects they can use as stamps.
2. If they do not use the stamps, how can they get a similar effect on the cushions?
3. What are primary, secondary and tertiary colours? Can they be mixed to make primary colours?
4. Discuss the mixing of primary colours to make secondary colours and so on.

Goals Achieved

- Enhanced attention span
- Better concept-building abilities
- Improved observation skills
- Develops persistence

Tick-tack Tips

1. Children can make patterns on their pillow covers with their names written on them using different designs.
2. Show them the mosaics made on tiles and discuss the ancient techniques and art forms.

Activity–27

Balloon Lampshades!

RESOURCES REQUIRED

- Balloons
- Strong transparent glue
- 8 to 10 metres of jute rope per balloon
- A pair of child-safe scissors
- Spray paint bottle

Getting Ready:

The balloon lampshade requires the child to fix the balloons on the lampshades. Parents need to ensure that all safety measures are taken before and during the activity.

Method:

1. Invite the children to take a balloon each, inflate it such that it stretches to its maximum and tie a knot to secure it.
2. Next, ask the children to pour the glue into a mixing bowl. Dip the jute rope into it such that the rope gets soaked in the glue completely.
3. Now, ask the children to stick the rope on top of the balloon. Begin wrapping the inflated balloon with the soaked rope. Leave a wide opening to insert the bulb into the lampshade.
4. The rope might slip a couple of times, but that is okay. However, if it slips too often then squeeze out the extra glue

from the rope.

5. Allow the jute rope to dry overnight. Now, poke the balloon with a pointed fork to burst it. Peel out the remains of the balloon. By now the dry rope would have hardened and taken the shape of the balloon.
6. Now, the rope is ready to be painted. Ask the children to use the spray paint to paint their respective balloon shaped ropes.
7. Supervise the children while they use the spray paint. Let the spray paint dry.
8. Next, instruct the children to wear rubber slippers before they place a bulb inside their lampshades. Ensure that the wire is unplugged.
9. Once the bulb has been fixed successfully, ask the child to switch on the lampshade.

Tickle the Thoughts:

1. What is light? What is the source of light?
2. How did people in ancient times live without electricity?
3. Is electricity the same as sunlight?

Goals Achieved

- Improved attention span
- Better observation abilities
- Explore and reformulate information
- Better motor skills

Tick-tack Tips

1. Children can tie the balloon's mouth on a water bottle's neck (which is full of water) to prevent it from flying away while they are working on it.
2. Some spray paints are also inflammable and toxic. Ensure that the children only use products that are safe to use.

Activity 28

Fly High—The Kites!

RESOURCES REQUIRED

- Kite paper
- Stickers
- String (manja)
- Glue
- A pair of child-safe scissors
- 2 garden stakes

Getting Ready:

1. Spare some extra time to fly the kite with the children.
2. The kite will fly more conveniently on a windy day.

Method:

1. Invite the children to take a square kite paper and cut it into a diamond shape. (Refer to the picture.)
2. Cut strips of kite paper to make the tail of the kite and stick them at point 'D'.
3. Ask them to stick different kinds of stickers on the kite and its tail.
4. Next, ask the children to take the stakes and make a 'cross'—AC and BD as shown in the picture, and tape the stakes down to secure them.
5. Help the children to thread the needle and pass it through

the stakes at the point 'O'. Ask them to thread the kite by sewing it diagonally such that the thread forms an 'X'—a multiplication sign. Now, ask the children to repeat the same at point 'P'.

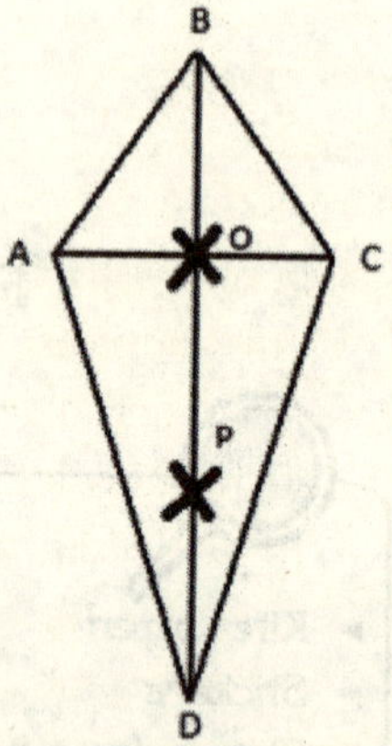

6. Ask them to pass a thread through the point 'O', leaving 8 to 10 inches of thread. Then pass the needle through the point 'P', leaving a long end of the thread. Tie a knot with the two long threads, forming a triangle.
7. Lifting up the kite, tie the *manja* to this triangle. The kite is ready to soar high up in the sky!

Tickle the Thoughts:

1. What is wind?
2. How does the direction of wind change?
3. Ask the children how they will know the direction of the wind when the kite is flying way up high in the sky.

Goals Achieved

- Improved attention span
- Better observation abilities
- Clearer perception
- Exercised fine motor skills

Tick-tack Tips

1. The tail of the kite indicates the direction of the wind while it is flying high.
2. If the kite sinks with its tail first, the wind is not sufficient for the kite to take flight.
3. The kites fly beautifully when the leaves of the trees are moving gently.

Activity–29

Paper Straw Letters!

RESOURCES REQUIRED

- Chart paper
- 4 to 5 newspapers
- A pair of child-safe scissors
- Glue

Getting Ready:

Keep the required resources ready.

Method:

1. Invite the children to take the newspapers and fold each of them into half, and yet another half to make it into a quarter and cut plenty of newspapers of equal lengths.
2. Ask the children to roll the newspapers into thin straws, preferably of equal thickness, to make them look even and neat.
3. Next, ask them to write the letters of the alphabet on the chart paper.
4. Using child-safe scissors, ask them to cut the newspaper straws into the required sizes and stick them in place using glue.

TIP: Try not to use too much glue to avoid an untidy look.

5. Once the glue dries, the paper straw letters are ready for display.

Tickle the Thoughts:

1. Ask the children if they would like to write a message to a friend using the straw letters.
2. What is paper made of? How is it made?
3. Explain the importance of trees to children.

Goals Achieved

- Enhanced attention span
- Exercised fine motor skills
- Clearer perception
- Helps in channelizing their energies and calming down

Tick-tack Tips

1. If time is a constraint, instead of making newspaper straws, children may use paper straws available in grocery stores.
2. Children can use one colour or multi-coloured straws.
3. Avoid using plastic straws as they are bad for the environment.

Activity–30

Pencil Organizer!

RESOURCES REQUIRED

- An empty tin can
- 1 Mod Podge
- A roll of jute
- 2 to 3 colours of acrylic paints
- 4 paintbrushes
- A pair of child-safe scissors

Getting Ready:

Ensure that the tin can does not have sharp edges.

Method:

1. Invite the children to paint a stripe of Mod Podge around the bottom of the tin can.
2. Help the children to wrap the jute rope over the tin can. Brush another stripe of Mod Podge and repeat the process until the can is fully covered with jute. Secure the ends of jute rope to prevent fraying.
3. Gently push the jute rope down after a few winds such that the tin is completely concealed. Repeat the process until the jute ropes reach the top edge of the tin, cut the rope at the end. Apply some extra Mod Podge to secure the jute ropes.
4. Choose two to three different poster colours, using

paintbrushes, paint the jute ropes in horizontal stripes in sets of three to four jute ropes per colour.

Tickle the Thoughts:

1. Ask the children what they would like to place in the organizer.
2. How does organizing things make life easier for them?
3. How would they organize their school bag?
4. Do they have the school's organizer (list of events)?

Goals Achieved

- Improved attention span
- Enhanced organization skills
- Better fine motor skills
- Encourages persistence to complete the task at hand

Tick-tack Tips

1. 'Organization' is a necessary skill that is required for the children to succeed in life. This activity gives parents an opportunity to explain the importance of 'organizational skills' to a young adult!
2. Jute has the tendency to absorb paint. Therefore, use acrylic paint liberally. If required, apply a second coat of paint on the previous stripe for the colours to look brilliant.

Activity–31

Votive Lace Candle Plates!

RESOURCES REQUIRED

- Acrylic paint and paintbrushes
- 1 PVA glue
- Decorations such as ribbons, laces, doilies, sequins
- Newspapers
- Metal lids

Getting Ready:

Keep some metal plates saved for reuse.

Method:

1. Cover the work surface with newspaper to protect it from paint stains.
2. Ask the children to paint the metal plates on both the sides. Let them dry.
3. Ask them to apply a second coat of acrylic paint on the plates. Let them dry again.
4. Ask the children to glue the doily on the inside of the plate.
5. Then, ask them to glue the lace on the edges of the plates.
6. Glue the sequin on the inside of the plate. Allow it to dry.
7. Place a battery-operated candle on the plate, and the plates are ready.

Tickle the Thoughts:

1. What are votive candles?
2. Ask the children how they would make votive candles.

Goals Achieved

- Improved attention span
- Improved association techniques
- Enhanced fine motor skills

Tick-tack Tips

1. Use clean and dry plates or lids to make votive candle plates.
2. Ensure that the metal plates do not have any sharp edges.

Activity–32

Embroidered Bottles!

RESOURCES REQUIRED

- 1 recyclable plastic bottle
- 1 roll of wool
- 1 needle
- 1 measuring tape
- A hole punch
- A pair of child-safe scissors
- A pencil for making the marks

Getting Ready:

Save the plastic bottles for recycling to make beautiful kitchen organizers!

Method:

1. Help the children to cut open a recyclable plastic bottle horizontally to the height they want.
2. Using a measuring tape, ask the children to measure the diameter of the bottle.
3. Leave about 1.5 cm from the top edge and help the children punch evenly spaced holes.
4. Encourage the children to thread the needle and sew the wool through the punched holes by going over and under the holes.

5. To hide the first knot, begin to sew from inside the bottle.
6. After the children have sewn the bottle, ask them to tie a knot to secure.

Tickle the Thoughts:

1. What is plastic?
2. What are biodegradables?
3. What is wool?

Goals Achieved

- Improved attention span
- Enhanced observation abilitie
- Enhanced fine motor skills

Tick-tack Tip

This activity encourages the children to reduce and reuse plastic. It is a good opportunity to explain the importance of recycling waste, and explaining the importance of conserving the environment.

Activity–33

Paper-clip Necklace!

RESOURCES REQUIRED

- 30 paper clips
- 1 roll of duct tape
- A pair of child-safe scissors

Getting Ready:

1. Keep a duct tape of 2 inches ready.
2. Cut 10 to 12 short strips of the tape measuring 1.8 cm each.

Paper clip

Method:

1. Help the children slip a paper clip into another to form a long chain of 25 to 30 pieces.
2. Ask them to stick the tapes around the joints of the chain such that the clips don't hurt the child.
3. The necklace of paperclips and tape is ready to be worn at a children's party.

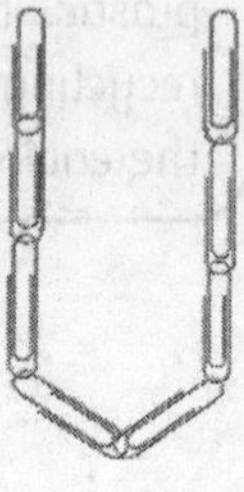

Goals Achieved

- Improved attention span
- Enhanced observation skills
- Better fine motor skills

Tick-tack Tip

Children can choose from a wide variety of tapes. The printed ones look pretty too.

Activity–34

Decorate the Fairy Lights!

RESOURCES REQUIRED

- 1 string of fairy lights
- 12 table tennis balls
- A pointed paper cutter

Getting Ready:

As the activity involves wires and electrical fittings, ask the children to wear rubber slippers and take necessary safety measures before and during the activity.

Method:

1. Help the children to use the paper cutter and make small incisions in the table tennis balls.
2. The incision should be large enough to insert one bulb of the fairy lights into one table tennis ball and small enough to secure the light from falling off.
3. Repeat it for the entire string of fairy lights. Fix the lights on the wall. Under adult supervision, help the child plug in the light and switch it on.

Tickle the Thoughts:

1. Ask the children how else they can decorate the lights.

2. Instead of table tennis balls, can they use lawn tennis balls? Why or why not?

Goals Achieved

- Improved attention span
- Enhanced fine motor skills
- Improved association abilities

Tick-tack Tip

Encourage children to decorate fairy lights using recyclable materials such as egg cartons.

Activity–35

Fairy Lights with Polka Dots!

RESOURCES REQUIRED

- Battery-operated fairy lights
- Paper cups 12 to 15 per fairy light
- 1 pencil
- Glue
- 1 paintbrush
- Coloured glazed paper
- A pair of child-safe scissors

Getting Ready:

Keep everything ready for use.

Method:

1. Using the child-safe scissors, ask the children to cut the glazed paper into circles with a diameter of 2.5 cm. These circles will look like polka dots when pasted on the cups.
2. Ask the children to apply glue on the paper cups using the paintbrush.
3. Ask them to take a pointed pencil and punch a hole at the bottom of the paper cup and remove the pencil.
4. Ask the children to push each bulb of the battery-operated fairy lights through the hole made in the paper cups. Now, help the children hang the lights wherever they choose to.

5. Then, ask them to place the battery inside the fairy light's circuit. Switch it on, and enjoy the colourful display of lights.

Tickle the Thoughts:

1. What is electricity?
2. What is a battery? Open the battery circuit for the children to explore.
3. How does a battery work?

Goals Achieved

- Increased attention span
- Better observation skills
- Enhanced fine motor skills
- Seek and explore possibilities

Tick-tack Tips

1. Children may use different shapes such as stars and hearts instead of circles.
2. Children can make holes at various places on the cup using a pencil. The light will pass through the holes and create a beautiful pattern.

Activity–36

Sock Mobile Covers!

RESOURCES REQUIRED

- 1 pair of socks
- 1 pair of child-safe scissors
- Needle and thread
- 1 black marker
- 12 buttons
- 10- to 12-cm-long piece of felt
- 1 measuring tape

Getting Ready:

Keep old socks to use later.

Method:

1. Invite the children to turn the pair of socks inside out. Slip in your cellphone into the socks until it reaches the ankle and not the foot.
2. On the calf of the sock, mark a line about 1.5 cm away from the top of the cellphone. Remove the phone from the sock. Help the children sew on this marked line, using the needle and thread, and cut off the foot of the sock.
3. Turn the sock inside out again such that the stitched portion remains inside.
4. Next, ask the children to press the sock down onto the work

surface to create a crease. Then, encourage them to sew the buttons on both the sides of the sock.

5. Now, cut a 2.5-inches-long strip of the felt. Stretch the felt till both the buttons on the sock; ask the children to use the measuring tape and help them carefully make small slits on the felt such that the buttons can pass through these slits. Insert your cellphone into the sock to check whether it fits perfectly. Button it up and the sock-mobile cover is ready for use.

Tickle the Thoughts:

1. What will happen if the felt is not measured properly?
2. Why do we need to cover the cell phone?

Goals Achieved

- Improved attention span
- Enhanced observation skills
- Exercised fine motor skills
- Developed numeracy skills

Tick-tack Tips

1. Children can stitch and decorate the sock mobile covers with pompoms as well.
2. Children may choose to make another sock-mobile cover using the other sock from the pair to gift to their friends.

Activity–37

Craft Stick Bracelets!

RESOURCES REQUIRED

- 1 craft stick
- 1 pan
- 250 ml of hot water
- 1 glass of water
- Glue

Getting Ready:

Keep a glass full of hot water ready for later use.

Method:

1. Invite the children to take a craft stick and place it in a pan of boiling water for 30 minutes so that it becomes soft and flexible.
2. As the water starts to boil, ensure that adults help the children pour the hot water into the pan. Allow it to cool down. Ask them to remove the craft stick from the water.
3. Now that the craft stick has become flexible, ask the children to place the stick horizontally into a glass to form a curve. Leave the stick to dry in the empty glass overnight.
4. Help the children apply glue on the inside of the curved stick and wind the embroidery threads tightly around the craft stick.

5. When the children want to add another thread of a different colour, ask them to tie it with the previous one, and shove the knot under the already wrapped threads to hide it. Finish the craft stick bracelets by securing the edges of the threads with glue.

Tickle the Thoughts:

1. What are threads made of?
2. Can we reuse human hair? If yes, how?

Goals Achieved

- Improved attention span
- Enhanced fine motor skills
- Clearer perception
- Encourages persistence

Tick-tack Tips

1. This activity helps the children understand the importance of animals and their products we can use. Children should be taught to love and care about animals.
2. This activity stretches over two days, encourage the children to be patient and persistent as good things take time.

Activity–38

Necklace with Hairgrips!

RESOURCES REQUIRED

- 100 hairgrips of different colours
- 1-metre-long jewellery wire
- 1 jewellery closure
- A pair of pliers
- Jump rings
- Wire clippers

Getting Ready:

Keep the required materials ready.

Method:

1. Invite the children to measure and cut 50- to 55-cm-long jewellery wire.
2. Ask them to slip in the hairgrips of different colours into the jewellery wire.
3. Encourage them to insert the jewellery closure at the left end of the wire and tie a knot.
4. Help the children wrap the ends of the wire by using the pliers to secure the closure.
5. Trim the excess wire using wire clippers so that the necklace does not have any sharp edges that may hurt the children.
6. At the right end of the wire, ask the children to insert the

jump ring and fold the wire over to secure the jump ring in place. Clip off any excess wire.

7. To secure the hairgrips in place, wrap a small piece of wire before the first and after the last hairgrip. Clip off any excess wire.

Tickle the Thoughts:

1. Ask the children how they can form patterns.
2. Where else can they decorate the hairgrips?
3. Can they enumerate five uses of hairgrips?

Goals Achieved

- Improved attention span
- Exercised fine motor skills
- Better numeracy skills
- Increased clarity about pattern making

Tick-tack Tip

This activity helps the children to form patterns and think out of the box. Encourage them to think about more uses of hairgrips.

Observation

Activity–39

Moon Chart!

RESOURCES REQUIRED

- Notebook for each child
- Pencils
- Erasers
- Rulers
- A clear night sky
- Newspapers

Getting Ready:

1. Check the weather for a clear sky on a full-moon night.
2. Go for a walk at night with the children.

Method:

1. Urge children to carry their notebooks, rulers, pencils and erasers.
2. Ask the children to draw 8 to 10 sections in their notebooks using their pencils and rulers.
3. Ask them to observe the moon and draw a picture of it in their notebooks, mentioning the date.
4. Take them out to observe the moon every third day. Tell them to study the moon and draw the changes observed.

Tickle the thoughts:

1. After a month's observation, ask the children to study and explain them to you.
2. Discuss the changes observed by them—the first quarter, half-moon and the full moon.
3. Explain to them the waxing and the waning moon.

Goals Achieved

- Enhanced observation abilities
- Better concept-building abilities
- Develops communication skills
- Better numeracy skills
- Associates and synthesizes information

Tick-tack-Tips

1. You may help children with Mnemonics to help them memorize a waxing or a waning moon. A waxing moon resembles the letter 'C.' The full moon looks like the letter 'O' and the waning moon looks similar to the letter 'D'.
2. You may help children make a graph showing the phases of the moon.

Activity–40

It's Raining, It's Pouring, but We Aren't Snoring!

RESOURCES REQUIRED

- 1 litre plastic bottle
- A pair of child-safe scissors
- 1 measuring tape
- 1 black marker
- Rain

Getting Ready:

Keep all the required resources in their respective quantities ready.

Method:

1. Ask the children to cut the one-litre bottle along its neck with the child-safe scissors, leaving the cylindrical part of the bottle wide open.
2. Next, ask the children to invert the cut out neck of the bottle to make a funnel. This funnel will prevent the water from evaporating. Invert it and place it on top of the bottle.
3. Using your measuring tape and black marker, ask the children to mark half inch-wide sections on the bottle. These marks will help them measure how much rain they have collected.

   TIP: An empty plastic bottle is very light in weight, and might fall down or fly away with the wind. Dig a hole in the ground and bury the lower end of the bottle. This will hold the bottle in place.

5. Then, ask the children to wait until the rain stops and then head out to check your gauge! Record your results.

Tickle the Thoughts:

1. Why is rain important? In which months does it rain?
2. Ask the children how can they measure rain. What is the unit of water?
3. Why do they need to measure the quantity of rainfall?
4. If they collect rainwater in a big barrel, how will they use the water?
5. What is rainwater harvesting?

Goals Achieved

- Better observation skills
- Improved association abilities
- Better concept-building abilities

Tick-tack Tips

1. You may explain the journey of rainwater to the ocean and discuss the names of various rivers and oceans of the world!
2. Discuss with children that water, on the way to the ocean, collects trash, chemicals, fertilizers and pollutants from the streets and rivers. This dirty water reaches the ocean, making the ocean dirty too. Ask the children how they can stop the pollutants from entering the oceans.

Activity–41

Marble Coasters!

RESOURCES REQUIRED

- 500 g of oven bake clay
- 1 cookie cutter
- 1 acrylic roller
- 1 paint pen
- Parchment paper

Getting Ready:

Keep all the required resources in their respective quantities ready.

Method:

1. Invite the children to take the oven bake clay. Ask them to roll out four long strings of different colours.
2. Next, take all the four strings and twist them together into one long thin string. The colours will blend but make sure that they do not turn into a greenish-gray colour.
3. Encourage them to make a ball and flatten it to a thickness of a quarter inch using the acrylic roller.
4. Use a cookie cutter to cut out shapes for the coaster.
5. Place the coasters on a parchment paper and bake at 275° for 25 to 30 minutes. Help the children remove them from the oven. Let them cool.
6. Give finishing touches to the coasters with the paint pen and

colour the edges. The coasters are ready for use!

Tickle the Thoughts:

1. Ask the children what else they can make using the same technique.
2. Ask them five different uses of the coaster they just made.
3. What happened when they placed the soft clay in the oven?

Goals Achieved

- Enhanced observation skills
- Improved sensory skills
- Better concept-building abilities

Tick-tack Tips

1. Since this activity involves the use of electronics, parents need to take all the necessary precautions to keep the children safe.
2. Help the child fix the temperature of the oven and remember to help them remove the baked coasters from the oven, as they will be hot.

Activity–42

Cement Pots!

RESOURCES REQUIRED

- 2 kg of white cement
- 1 litre of water
- 4 mixing bowls
- 4 big empty plastic bowls
- 4 small empty plastic bowls
- 2 paintbrushes
- 250 g of vegetable oil
- 1 apron
- 1 pair of gloves

Getting Ready:

1. Cover the table with a newspaper before the children start making the pots.
2. Ensure that the children wear aprons and gloves.

Method:

1. Invite the children to apply vegetable oil on the outside of the small bowls, using the broad paintbrushes. Ask the children to take a mixing bowl and put 1.5 kg of cement into it. Add 500 ml of water to the cement and mix them well so that there are no lumps. Add water, a little at a time, to get a pouring consistency, like that of a cake batter.

2. Now, ask the children to apply oil on the inside of the bigger bowl and pour the cement mixture into it. Do not fill it up to the brim, as it will spill over when you place the smaller bowl inside it.
3. Place the smaller bowl into the bigger one to give the cement the shape of a bowl. Put a weight in the small bowl to stop it from moving until the cement dries up. This usually takes four to five hours.
4. Once the cement has dried up, remove the smaller bowl, and turn the bigger bowl upside down. Now, remove the bigger bowl as well. The new white cement pot is ready to be painted!
5. Encourage the children to paint the cemented pots using acrylic colours.

Tickle the Thoughts:

1. What is cement?
2. Why did the cement become hard when it dried up?
3. Ask the children what their houses, or the buildings surrounding them, are made of.

Goals Achieved

- Better observation skills
- Improved sensory skills
- A better sense of achievement

Tick-tack Tips

1. Children may add one portion of Plaster of Paris to four portions of cement to work on designs that are more intricate. This gives the children more time to work before the cement dries up.
2. Children may use the regular grey cement instead of the white cement.
3. Help the children to sow seeds in the garden. Once the plants grow, scoop them out, and place them in a cement pot.

Activity–43

Pot Decorations!

RESOURCES REQUIRED

- 1 pot
- 25 to 30 wooden cloth pegs
- 3 to 4 plastic cups

Getting Ready

Ask the children to choose the plastic cups that would fit into the flower pots to be decorated.

Method:

1. Ask the children to take one wooden cloth peg at a time and fix it at the mouth of their respective plastic cups. They should be placed in such a way that there is no space between two pegs.
2. Next, help the children to cut the plastic cups horizontally into two halves.
3. Now, ask the children to place the plastic cups inside the flower pots.

Tickle the Thoughts:

1. How else can you decorate the flower pots?
2. Would you like to grow plants in the pots? Give it a try!

Goals Achieved

- Improved association skills
- Ability to synthesize information
- Enhanced fine motor skills

Tick-tack Tips

1. Children may decorate the pots using jute ropes and aluminium foil.
2. Tie a rubber band around the pegs; it will help the children secure the pegs better.

Activity–44

Bookmarks!

RESOURCES REQUIRED

- Different textured tree barks
- 1 PVA glue
- 1 glue stick
- 1 A4-sized paper
- A pair of child-safe scissors
- 1 box of wax crayons
- 1 hole punch
- 1-metre-long ribbon or string

Getting Ready:

Keep some extra time to go outdoors with the children to collect natural waste such as textured tree barks, leaves, flower petals, etc.

Method:

1. Ask the children to cut the A4-sized paper into different shapes using child-safe scissors.
2. Now, ask them to place the paper on a tree's bark and rub the wax crayon on the paper. The grooves of the bark will make a pattern on the paper.
3. Next, they may use the hole punch to make a hole in the paper to thread a ribbon or a string through it. To further decorate the bookmark, stick small bits of the bark on it.

Tickle the Thoughts:

1. What are bookmarks used for?
2. How else can they trace patterns on paper?
3. Ask the children about other methods to make bookmarks.
4. What else can they use instead of the textured barks?

Goals Achieved

- Enhanced observation skills
- Improved association abilities
- Improved sensory skills

Tick-tack Tips

1. You may write a nice message on the bookmark for the reader of the book to read.
2. Urge the children not to rub the wax crayons too hard on the paper, as it might tear the paper.

Activity–45

Flower Press Greeting Cards!

RESOURCES REQUIRED

- 4 flowers
- A ball-shaped paper weight
- 1 wooden board
- Watercolour paper
- 2 sheets of tracing paper
- Ribbons

Getting Ready:

Go to the garden with the children to pick beautiful and fresh flowers such as cosmos, hibiscus and pansies.

Method:

1. Invite the children to place a wooden board on the work surface, and fix the watercolour paper on it.
2. Ask the children to place the flower facing down on the watercolour paper.
3. Ask the children to place the tracing paper on top of the flower. Gently roll the paperweight on the tracing paper. This will squeeze out the juices from the flower and leave an imprint on the paper.
4. Allow it to dry.

5. Now, remove the flower, punch a hole into the paper and tie a ribbon.

Tickle the Thoughts:

1. Ask the children how the watercolour paper got the imprints from the flower.
2. Will the flowers make imprints on plastic? Why or why not?
3. Why did we cover the flower with tracing paper?

Goals Achieved

- Better observation skills
- Enhanced association abilities
- Clearer perception
- Refined motor skills

Tick-tack Tips

1. Ensure that the paperweight does not have pointed edges or is not broken, as it might tear the tracing paper and damage the flowers imprint.
2. Children may make greeting cards to send to their friends and relatives.

Activity–46

Bottle Decorations!

RESOURCES REQUIRED

- 1 glass bottle
- 1 PVA glue
- 4 candles

Getting Ready:

Go to the garden with children to pick beautiful and fresh leaves.

Method:

1. Invite the children to take a clean glass bottle and apply a coat of glue on it.
2. Ask them to press the leaves gently onto the surface of the glass such that the leaves take the shape of the bottle. Ensure that there are no air bubbles.
3. Ask the children to apply another coat of glue. Allow it to dry until the glue turns transparent.
4. Now, help the children to place a candle inside the bottle and light it.

Tickle the Thoughts:

1. What else can be placed inside the bottles instead of candles?
2. What else can we paste on the bottle?

Goals Achieved

- Improved observation skills
- Better association abilities
- Enhanced fine motor skills

Tick-tack Tips

1. You can place colourful fairy lights inside the bottle.
2. Ask children to look for leaves of different colours and shapes.
3. Children may also use fresh and colourful petals of different kinds of flowers.

Activity–47

Mug Wall Hangings!

RESOURCES REQUIRED

- An old mug
- 1 kg of Plaster of Paris
- 1 pair of gloves
- 1 apron
- 1 small box of petroleum jelly
- 1 packet of glitter
- 1 empty plastic container
- 1 sheet of soft sand paper
- 3 to 4 synthetic enamel boxes
- Paintbrush

Getting Ready:

Ask the children to wear gloves and aprons before they begin the activity.

Method:

1. Invite the children to take an old, clean mug.
2. Encourage them to find an old plastic container which is big enough to fit the mug.
3. Ask the children to liberally apply petroleum jelly on the insides of the container. Ask them to add Plaster of Paris to that container and pour water, little by little, stirring it constantly.

4. Once all the lumps have dissolved and the mixture has a pouring consistency, help the children dip only the broken side of the mug into it. Let it dry for five to six hours.
5. Gently tap the container on the outside to loosen the Plaster of Paris. Remove the mug along with Plaster of Paris from the container. The broken side of the mug is now covered with Plaster of Paris.
6. Next, ask the children to smoothen the Plaster of Paris using the sand paper.
7. Once the surface is smooth, apply synthetic enamel.
8. Children may sprinkle glitter if they wish to. Let it dry.
9. Once it is dry, using the paintbrush, urge the children to apply varnish to give it a glossy finishing touch.

Tickle the Thoughts:

1. Ask the children how they can recycle broken materials.
2. What else can we do to make the new mug look good?
3. Why should they recycle material?

Goals Achieved

- Improved attention span
- Better observation skills
- Enhanced sensory skills
- Helps to understand 'reduce waste' and 'recycle the resources'

Tick-tack Tips

1. Place some artificial flowers in the mug and hang it as a wall hanging!
2. It can also be used as a kitchen organizer.

Activity–48

Glittering Gift Boxes!

RESOURCES REQUIRED

- 1 empty carton
- Newspapers
- 2 to 3 acrylic paints
- 1 to 2 paintbrushes
- 1 glue
- 1 packet of glitter
- 10 bindis
- 1-metre-long ribbon

Getting Ready:

Cover the work surface with newspaper.

Method:

1. Invite the children to choose a carton to create a glittering gift box.
2. Urge them to paint the the gift box using the acrylic paint and paintbrushes.
3. Encourage them to paint interesting shapes of their choice and let them dry.
4. Ask the children to apply glue and sprinkle glitter liberally over the glue. Leave the box to dry overnight. Apply colourful bindis on the box.

5. Encourage the children to pack a gift in the box and tie it with a ribbon. The 'Glittering Gift Box' is ready.
6. Encourage the children to hand over the box to their peers.

Tickle the Thoughts:

1. What other material can one use to decorate gift boxes?
2. How can one make occasion-specific gift boxes?

Goals Achieved

- Better concept-building abilities
- Increased thinking skills
- Enhanced social skills

Tick-tack Tips

1. You can use different colours for different occasions such as red and yellow for Diwali, and red, green and white for making gift boxes for Christmas.
2. If time permits, you can ask the children to cut and paste different shapes of crepe paper instead of using bindis.

Activity–49

Mother Earth Collage!

RESOURCES REQUIRED:

- 4 thin tree barks
- 1 PVA glue
- 1 glue stick
- 1 old magazine
- 1 chart paper
- Natural waste such as feathers, dry flowers, leaves, dead insects, etc.

Getting Ready:

Take out some extra time to go with the children to explore nature and collect natural waste.

Method:

1. Encourage the children to decide on a theme and cut out pictures from magazines. For example, a jungle.
2. Invite the children to cut tree barks using a child-safe scissors into four equal lengths.
3. Using the PVA glue, ask them to stick barks to form corners. Join all the corners to form a frame.
4. Ask them to cut the chart paper as per the size of the frame and stick their collection on the chart paper.

5. Help them to stick the frame on the chart paper such that the collage is clearly visible inside the frame.

Tickle the Thoughts:

1. Ask the children which theme they would prefer.
2. What materials would they like to collect and where can they find them?
3. What is natural waste?
4. Why do they need to conserve the natural environment?

Goals Achieved

- Better observation skills
- Improved association abilities
- Helps to perceive things differently

Tick-tack Tip

This activity gives parents the time to join their children and get closer to nature. Talk to the children about the natural treasures that the beautiful world has in store for them. Take this opportunity to inculcate in children the love for nature. Encourage them to keep the natural environment safe from felling trees and damaging plants.

Activity–50

Candle Stand–I!

Players: 1 to 2

RESOURCES REQUIRED

- 1 to 2 glass bowls
- 1 cellophane roll
- 1 PVA glue
- Colourful pebbles

Getting Ready:

Cut the cellophane big enough to cover the glass bowl from inside till its brim.

Method:

1. Take the pebbles one at a time and place them inside the bowl such that they form another layer inside it.
2. Now apply the glue to each pebble. Allow them to dry.
3. Pick up the new bowl of pebbles gentaly and remove the cellophane.
4. Place the candle in the new candle stand and help children light it.

Tickle the Thoughts:

1. Ask the children what other materials they can use to make the candle stand.
2. Ask them how else they can decorate the candles.
3. What is light and what is shadow?

Goals Achieved

- Increased span of concentration
- Enhanced thinking skills
- Better fine motor skills
- Encourages creativity
- Better observation skills

Tick-tack Tips

1. Preferably, use pebbles that have a flat base so that they balance well in the bowl.
2. You can recycle old toys such as building blocks to make soap cases in a similar way.

Activity–51

Candle Stands–II!

RESOURCES REQUIRED

- 1 empty broad-based bottle
- Strong adhesive
- Dry leaves
- 5 to 6 candles
- 1-metre-long jute rope

Getting Ready:

Go to the garden with the children to pick some dry leaves.

Method:

1. Invite the children to take their bottles and apply glue on the outer walls of the bottles.
2. Ask the children to stick the leaves on the bottles and apply glue on the leaves and the bottle once again. Let it dry.
3. Apply some glue at the neck and the bottom of the bottle. Wind and stick the jute rope around the neck and the bottom of the bottle.
4. Ask the children to leave a three-inch gap at the middle of the bottle from where the candle's light will emanate. Let it dry.
5. Now, place the candles inside the bottle and light them.

Tickle the Thoughts:

1. What else can be added to the bottle to make it look pretty?
2. How else can we use this candle stand?

Goals Achieved

- Enhanced association abilities
- Improved sensory skills
- Clearer perception
- Better observation skills

Tick-tack Tips

1. Encourage children to go for a field trip to a botanical garden to pick dry natural leaves and twigs that can be used for decoration.
2. Collect twigs from the garden and cut them into equal sizes. Tie them on the outer side of the bottle. Pour sand into the bottle and place a candle.

Activity–52

Hand-painted Gift Wraps!

RESOURCES REQUIRED

- 12 poster colours
- 2 paintbrushes
- 1 colouring palette
- 1 toilet paper roll
- 10 to 12 stickers
- 1 child-safe knife
- 1 pencil with eraser for each child
- 1 sheet of bubble wrap paper
- 1 wax seal

Getting Ready:

Cover the work surface before starting the activity.

Method:

Example 1:

1. Encourage the children to cut the cardboard roll inside the toilet paper roll into rings of 4 cm each.
2. Urge the children to dip the rings in the colour palette and print them on the chart paper.
3. Children may stick stickers on the chart paper inside each ring.

Example 2:

1. Ask the children to take a chart paper, and cut out different shapes such as ovals, water droplets and stars, etc., using the child-safe knife.
2. Next, ask them to place this chart paper on top of another chart paper. Paint the shapes with poster colours.

Example 3:

1. Encourage the children to take a pencil that has a small eraser attached at its end.
2. Ask the children to dip the eraser into the colour palette. Stamp it on the chart paper to make small and beautiful polka dots.

Example 4:

1. Invite the children to take a sheet of bubble wrap, and brush poster colour over the bubble wrap. Press it down on a chart paper.
   The colour from the bubble wrap paper will be imprinted on the chart paper. Allow the colour to dry and only then gently remove the bubble wrap.

Example 5:

1. Ask the children to take a wax seal and dip it in different colours. Stamp it on the chart paper forming different patterns.

Tickle the Thoughts:

1. Ask the children why they should wrap gifts.
2. Should their friends open the gifts in front of them? Why or why not?

Goals Achieved

- Improved attention span
- Enhanced association abilities
- Better social skills

Tick-tack Tips

1. This activity gives a good opportunity to parents to discuss appropriate social behaviour with children. Encourage them to think and come up with a set of acceptable and not-acceptable rules.
2. Children can be asked to go around the house and find interesting objects that can be used for stamping.

Activity–53

Pour the Paint Pots!

RESOURCES REQUIRED

- 1 transparent pot
- 1 kitchen funnel
- 1 box of poster paints

Getting Ready:

Clean and dry the glass pots before use.

Method:

1. Invite the children to take the transparent pots and pour poster colours into them using a kitchen funnel.
2. Ask the children to rotate and tilt the pots such that the paint flows and it coats the inside walls of the pots completely. Let them dry.
3. Encourage children to experiment colouring the pots using different colours.
4. The 'Pour the Paint Pots' are ready to be decorated with beautiful flowers.

Tickle the Thoughts:

1. Ask the children how else they can decorate the pots.
2. What else can they put inside the pots?
3. What will happen if two colours are mixed in the pots?

4. Which colour will they get by mixing green and blue? Change the colours to develop a conversation with the children.

Goals Achieved

- Improved observation skills
- Enhanced curiosity
- Better attention span

Tick-tack Tips

1. Children may tie a ribbon around the neck of the pots, stick sequins and glitter to add variety in terms of design to the pots!
2. Children may add texture to the paint for a different look.

Association

Activity–54

Edible Christmas-Door Wreath!

RESOURCES REQUIRED

- 1 wire coat-hanger
- 2-metre-long string
- 2 packets of candies
- 1-meter-long ribbon

Getting Ready:

By the looks of the wreath, you may expect more guests this time for Christmas. Prepare in advance!

Method:

1. Invite the children to bend a metal coat-hanger into a circle.
2. Ask them to stick leaves and cherries on the coat-hanger.
3. Help them tie the candies to a string and stick it on the coat hanger such that the children can easily pull out the candies.
4. To give the wreath a professional touch, tie a ribbon on top of the coat hanger.
5. Hang the beautiful Christmas wreath on the door.

Tickle the Thoughts:

1. Ask the children why they need to decorate the main entrance of our home. Can there be a story behind hanging a wreath at the door?

2. How else can they make wreaths for the door?

Goals Achieved

- Enhanced association abilities
- Improved social skills
- Better aesthetic skills

Tick-tack Tip

Children can make a wreath using marshmallows of different colours.

Activity–55

The Mummy!

RESOURCES REQUIRED

- 4 to 6 rolls of toilet paper
- 5 glue sticks
- 1 box of poster colours
- 5 paintbrushes
- 1 stopwatch

Getting Ready:

Tell the children a story about mummifying in Egypt. Try not to scare them by adding an element of fun to the story.

Method:

1. Invite children to make teams of three players.
2. Ask one child in each team to play the role of a mummy.
3. Set the stopwatch to five minutes and ask the children to create the mummy.
4. Ask the child to stand with his or her arms stretched out and legs apart. Ask the other teammates to take the toilet paper rolls and begin wrapping the child with them.
5. Children can apply poster colours on the wrapped toilet paper to give the mummy a scary look!
6. The first team to complete the mummy wins the game. Ask the children to ensure that no part of their skin or clothes

is exposed.

7. Ask the mummy to role-play the dead, and scare the opponent teams!

Tickle the Thoughts:

1. What is the difference between being dead and alive?
2. How are dead bodies preserved?
3. Who are zombies?

Goals Achieved

- Enhanced association abilities
- Increased reasoning skills
- Promotes communication skills

Tick-tack Tips

1. To make the mummy look scarier, switch off the lights of the room and give the teams a torch to be placed right under the face of the mummy!
2. This activity gives parents an opportunity to help children understand life, death and ghosts. When children hear ghost stories at their age, they begin to fear. This is when parents should guide and address their curiosities and concerns in the right way and at the right time. Certain things, when explained properly to children by adults they trust, can help them become more confident and not get frightened when their friends talk about ghosts and tell ghost stories.

Activity–56

Smiley Egg Shell Candles!

RESOURCES REQUIRED

- 2 pans–one larger than the other
- 1 litre of water
- 2 eggs
- 500 g of paraffin wax
- A thread to make the wick
- 2 pencils
- 1 marker

Getting Ready:

1. Take the bigger pan, pour the water into it and bring it to the boil.
2. Take the smaller pan and add paraffin wax into it. Place this pan inside the larger pan of boiling water. Wait for the wax to melt. The heat from the first pan will melt the wax in the second pan. The molten wax is ready for use.

Method:

1. At the tip of the eggs, help the children to make a small hole in the shells and emply them into a bowl.
2. Help the children to wrap the thread around a pencil for each egg shell. Leave the thread long enough to reach the base of the egg to form the wick.

3. Next, with an adult's supervision, help the children pour the molten wax into the empty egg shells.
4. Allow the eggs to cool. Remove the pencils and cut the extra thread of the wick.
5. Now, gently tap the egg shells and peel them off.
6. The 'egg candles' can be decorated using permanent markers. The candles are ready for use. Light them when required.

Goals Achieved

- Enhanced association skills
- Better observation skills
- Exercised fine motor skills
- Improved sensory skills

Tick-tack Tips

1. Collect old twigs from the garden, and help the children to place them aesthetically around the candles to give them a finished look.
2. Keep the eggs in the egg tray during the activity.

Activity–57

Papier-mâché!

RESOURCES REQUIRED

- 2 glass bowls
- 1 small box of petroleum jelly
- 1 tissue paper roll
- 1 box of poster colours
- 2 paintbrushes
- 1-metre-long cord
- 1 roll of masking tape
- 1 PVA glue

Getting Ready:

Keep the required resources ready for making papier-mâché.

Method:

1. Invite the children to take their glass bowls (moulds) and ask them to apply a coat of petroleum jelly with their fingers on the inner walls of their bowls.
2. Next, ask the children to take another bowl and mix the PVA glue with water in a ratio of 50:50 to make a fine solution.
3. Now, ask the children to apply a layer of tissue paper and the solution alternately inside the glass bowl. Apply at least four to five layers of each. Let it dry overnight.
4. Help the children to slip out the papier-mâché bowl from

the glass bowl gently.

5. Help them use the masking tape to stick a cord on the rim of the bowl to secure it.
6. Now, ask the children to use poster colours to paint the bowl in vibrant colours.

Tickle the Thoughts:

1. What else can be made using papier-mâché? Ask the children to go around the house to look for similar things to use as moulds.
2. What was the special property of the toilet paper for making papier-mâché?
3. How did a soft paper turn into a hard bowl?
4. Which other recyclable paper can be used in place of toilet paper?

Goals Achieved

- Enhanced association abilities
- Clearer concept of 'recycling the material'
- Exercised fine motor skills
- Improved sensory skills

Tick-tack Tips

1. Children can make tie boxes for their father on his birthday and jewellery boxes for Mother's Day using this technique!
2. Children may stick beads and use glitter to make the papier-mâché boxes look more attractive.

Activity–58

Bottle-lid Decorations!

RESOURCES REQUIRED

- 4 to 5 old artificial flowers
- 500 g gypsum powder
- 1 litre of water
- 2 bowls
- 5 to 6 bottle lids to be decorated
- Strong adhesive

Getting Ready:

Keep old artificial flowers and empty bottles that you were planning to discard, ready for a new look.

Method:

1. Invite the children to take an empty bowl, pour two tablespoons of gypsum powder into it. Add some water and make a smooth paste.
2. Next, dip the artificial flowers in the solution.
3. Remove the flowers from the solution and let them dry.
4. Take the dry flowers, apply glue to the flowers and place them on the lids of the bottles. Let them dry.
5. Ask the children to use acrylic colours to paint the flowers as per their choices.

Tickle the Thoughts:

1. Ask the children where can they place the flowers.
2. Ask them if they can decorate the lids of the bottles with natural dry plants.

Goals Achieved

- Enhanced association abilities
- Increased visualization skills
- Improved observation skills
- Enhanced creativity

Tick-tack Tip

Encourage children to go for a field trip to a botanical garden to pick dry natural plants that can be used for decoration.

Activity–59

The Family Tree!

RESOURCES REQUIRED

- A pair of child-safe scissors
- 1 PVA glue
- 1 photo frame
- Thin twigs and branches that will fit the frame
- 5-metre-long thread
- Pictures of family members
- A double-sided tape
- Card paper
- Chart paper
- 1-metre-long thin wire

Getting Ready:

1. Search the old family albums for photographs of ancestors.
2. Teach the children to handle the photographs with utmost care.
3. Go outdoors with the children to collect some twigs and branches.

Method:

1. Invite the children to take a photo frame and fix a thin tree branch between the cardboard cover at the back and the wooden frame.

2. Help them cut the wires and tie the branches of the twig by poking holes through the cardboard cover. Twist the wires behind the cardboard cover to secure the branches.
3. Using the child-safe scissors, cut the card paper into pieces as per the sizes of the photographs.
4. Ask the children to cut small pieces of double-sided tape and stick them on the card paper.
5. Ask them to place the photographs carefully on the cards. The photograph-cards are ready; keep them aside.
6. Take the leaves and place them over the chart paper, draw the outlines of the leaves and cut the chart paper accordingly. Cut plenty of leaves to fill up the family tree. Colour the leaves and stick them on the branches using the masking tape.
7. The photograph-cards are ready to be stuck on the family tree. Ask them to cut three inches of masking tape and wrap it around the index and the tall finger to form a loop. Take it out, stick it behind the card paper, and place it on the tree.
8. Help the children to write the names of the family members under their photographs.

Tickle the Thoughts:

1. What is a family?
2. Who were our ancestors? (Help the children associate themselves to the family.)
3. Why is it called a family tree? Suggest a different name for the family tree. Why do we have 'last names' attached to our first names?

Goals Achieved

- Enhanced association abilities
- Better understanding of family ties
- Better observation skills
- Exercised fine motor skills

Tick-tack Tips

1. Talk to the children about your family during the activity. It is a good opportunity for the parents to discuss the traditions followed by the family over generations, which have helped them to stay close together.
2. Explain to the children how they are associated to the other members of the family and how important they are for the whole family.
3. Display the child's work somewhere, which is clearly visible. When the child is upset or experiencing failures in life, these pictures and your encouraging conversation will help the child to pull himself or herself together and face the challenges with a renewed strength.

Activity–60

Wax Resist Book Covers!

RESOURCES REQUIRED

- 8 to 10 leaves with deep grooves
- 1 box of wax crayons
- 50 ml of ink
- 2 card papers
- 1 paintbrush
- 1 pair of child-safe scissors

Getting Ready:

Keep some extra time to go to the garden with the children to pick up beautiful leaves, especially the textured ones and those with grooves.

Method:

1. Invite the children to take card paper as big as the book and press the leaf down on it. Ask them to trace the outline of the leaf with a lead pencil.
2. Ask the children to remove the leaf from the paper and draw over the pencil's outline using a crayon.
3. Children may add a few extra strokes with the crayons to give the leaf some dimension.
4. Ask the children to dip the paintbrush into the ink and brush over the leaf drawn on the paper. Let it dry.

5. Help them use the sheets to cover the book as per their requirements.

Tickle the Thoughts:

1. Ask the children why the ink brushed over the crayon's sketch did not mix with the colours of the crayons.
2. What else can be used instead of leaves?

Goals Achieved

- Enhanced association abilities
- Better concept-building skills
- Enhanced observation skills
- Clearer perception

Tick-tack Tips

1. Children may cut out lots of leaves made during the activity and stick them closely together. Stick them on the notebook to give the book an artistic look.
2. The crayons are waterproof and hence the crayons and the ink do not mix.

Activity–61

Rocks' Rock!

RESOURCES REQUIRED

- 1 PVA glue
- 6 poster colours
- 2 paintbrushes
- 10 shells
- Decorations such as googly eyes and glitter
- 1 tin
- 1 enamel paint

Getting Ready:

Take a walk in the garden with the children and collect smooth pebbles such as the ones found on riverbeds.

Method:

Example 1:

Ask the children to choose the stones, and using poster colours and paintbrushes, paint the stone blue, resembling the colour of the sea. Let it dry and then ask the children to stick the shells on them using the PVA glue.

Example 2:

Ask the children to choose oval-shaped rocks, starting from bigger rocks to the smaller ones. Ask them to stick the rocks using PVA glue and pile them up. Stick them in the increasing order of their size. Let the glue dry. Now, ask the children to pour the poster colours on the pile of rocks. Let it dry. Place them in the balcony.

Example 3:

Using poster colours, paint polka dots on the rocks. Polka dots look very colourful as they add a lot of colour to dark corners of the house.

Example 4:

Take a tin can and paint it with the enamel paint. Allow it to dry. Next, ask the children to paint the rocks in different colours. Let them dry. Now, using the PVA glue, ask them to stick the rocks on the tin.

Example 5:

Mix and match rocks of different shapes and sizes to make them look like animals. Paint the rocks as per the colour of the animal. Use PVA glue to stick googly eyes on the rocks.

Tickle the Thoughts:

1. What are rocks?
2. How are they formed?
3. What are the different kinds of rocks?

Goals Achieved

- Enhanced association abilities
- Enhanced observation skills
- Improved fine motor skills
- Better concept building abilities

Tick-tack Tips

1. Children can go outdoors and collect lots of rocks and pebbles, and make huge animals such as dinosaurs on the ground.
2. Encourage children to build houses; help them get bricks and cement to help them associate and get a feel of how different materials are used to construct houses.

Activity–62

Wooden Vase!

RESOURCES REQUIRED

- 2 empty tins
- 1 PVA glue
- Twigs
- 3 rubberbands
- Dry natural plants
- 1-metre-long ribbon

Getting Ready:

1. Go outdoors with children to collect twigs.
2. Cut the twigs into equal sizes. The twigs should be as tall as the tin.

Method:

1. Invite the children to erect the twigs and tie them around the tin using rubber bands.
2. Ask the children to apply the PVA glue to stick the twigs firmly to the tin and remove the rubber bands.
3. Place beautiful flowers in the tin.
4. Ask children to stick dry natural plants such as seedpods, pinecones around the twigs.
5. The 'Wooden Vase' is ready to be displayed.

Tickle the Thoughts:

1. Ask the children where they would like to place the vase.
2. How else can they decorate the vase?
3. Discuss the life cycle of plants with the children.

Goals Achieved

- Enhanced association skills
- Clearer perception
- Improved fine motor skills

Tick-tack Tips

1. If you have extra twigs left, make a photo frame.
2. Children can also grow their own plants and later place them in the vase!

Activity–63

Rag Mod Podge Bowl!

RESOURCES REQUIRED

- 1 bowl (narrow-bottomed and wide-mouthed)
- Scrap fabric
- 1 Mod Podge
- 1 plastic wrap
- A pair of child-safe scissors

Getting Ready:

The bowl should not have grooves on it.

Method:

1. Ask the children to take a piece of scrap fabric and a bowl.
2. Cut strips of rags about 2.5 cm wide and long enough to go around the circumference of the bowl. The lengths of the strips will vary depending upon the circumference of the bowl, where children want to paste the strips. Cut the fabric into 8 to 10 strips.
3. Ask the children to wrap the outer side of the bowl with plastic and secure the ends of the plastic by folding them towards the (inner) centre of the bowl. This will protect the bowl from Mod Podge. Turn the bowl upside down.
4. Next, ask the children to apply Mod Podge liberally on the outer side of the bowl.

5. Then, ask them to take the fabric, which will form the first innermost layer of the finished bowl. Place the fabric on the bowl with the front side of the fabric facing the bowl.
6. Apply Mod Podge at the centre of the bowl and begin sticking the fabric.

   TIP: To form the base of the rag mod podge bowl, a square piece of fabric provides adequate support.

7. Ask the children to press the fabric down gently with their hands. Paste the strips one by one beginning at the bottom edge of the bowl. The strips should fill-up any gap that is left exposed.
8. Encourage children to apply 3 to 4 layer of strips the same way, and set aside to dry for a day.
9. Trim the extra fabric to finish the beautiful bowl.

Tickle the Thoughts:

1. Ask the children to go around the house and get more such objects that can be made more beautiful using this technique.
2. Ask them what they would look for in those objects.

Goals Achieved

- Enhanced association abilities
- Improved attention span
- Enhanced observation skills
- Improved fine motor skills

Tick-tack Tips

1. Children may place their favourite objects in the bowls, or they may gift the bowl to their friends on their birthdays by making Rag Mod Podge Bowls specific for the occasions.
2. If the bowl is bigger, the fabric and the strips required will vary.

Activity–64

Old Tee's Bag!

RESOURCES REQUIRED

- 1 old t-shirt
- 1 pair of child-safe scissors

Getting Ready:

Keep some old t-shirts ready for recycling.

Method:

1. Ask the children to go and find some old t-shirts in their cupboards.
2. Encourage them to fold the t-shirt vertically into half with its right side out.
3. Next, ask them to cut out the t-shirt's neck and the arm such that the t-shirt looks like a vest with a deep neck and back. This will make the loops of the bag. Keep the cutout fabric for use later.
4. Ask them to invert the t-shirt inside out, and at the waist of the t-shirt, take the cutout armhole's fabric and tie a knot to secure the end. This will make the base of the bag.
5. Again, invert the t-shirt. The bag is ready for use!

Tickle the Thoughts:

1. Ask the children how they can recycle old clothes.
2. Why is recycling so important?

Goals Achieved

- Enhanced association abilities
- Improved attention span
- Better ability to follow multiple-step instructions

Tick-tack Tips

This activity gives parents an opportunity to encourage the children to reuse and recycle objects. Explain the importance of conserving the environment and its resources.

Activity–65

Fashion Footwear!

RESOURCES REQUIRED

- Slippers/floaters/canvas shoes
- Laces and fur
- Googly eyes
- Sequins, beads and artificial flowers to match the party attire
- A pair of child-safe scissors
- 1 can of PVA glue

Getting Ready:

Save the boring footwear to transform it into a style statement at a birthday party.

Method:

Boring Ballerina Shoes:
Take the shoes and using PVA glue stick some matching fur on top of them.

Old Thigh-high Boots:
Invite the children to use the PVA glue and stick some matching shoe frills.

Flip Flops:

Appliqué the flip-flops with artificial flowers and fruits using the PVA glue.

Slip-on Loafers:

Using the PVA glue, stick some googly eyes on the slip-ons and make a design with craft pens of different colours.

Classy Oxfords:

Using PVA glue, stick lace on the shoes to give them a fresh classy look.

Casual Crocs:

Ask the children to stick some amazing flowers on their casual crocs with PVA glue.

Tickle the Thoughts:

1. Why do people wear footwear? Discuss the importance of good footwear.
2. What are the different parts of a shoe?
3. When were shoes invented?

Goals Achieved

- Enhanced association abilities
- Improved fine motor skills
- Increased concentration span
- Enhanced visualization skills

Tick-tack Tips

1. Discuss the episode from the *Ramayana* where Bharat got Ram's footwear from the jungle.
2. Allow children to get creative with their designs to give the old shoes a new look.

Activity–66

Gift-wrapping Papers!

RESOURCES REQUIRED

- 2 to 3 colours of acrylic paint
- 3 mixing bowls
- 2 to 3 corncobs
- 3 chart papers (different colours)
- 2-metre-long ribbon
- 1 glue stick
- 6 doilies
- 2 handmade paper sheets (red and yellow) depending on the size of the gift
- 2-metre-long *mauli* (red coloured thread)
- 2 transparent tape
- 4 bowls
- 3 poster colours
- 5 to 6 sponge pieces
- 1 pair of child-safe scissors
- 2 coloured crepe papers
- 2 pipe cleaners

Getting Ready:

Keep the required resources ready.

Method:

Let us make different types of gift-wrapping papers:

Type 1:

1. Invite the children to choose the colour of chart paper to make the gift-wrapping paper with.
2. Ask the children to pour acrylic paint into the bowls.
3. Give them corncobs and ask them to dip them in paint and roll the corncobs on the chart paper. Let it dry.

Type 2:

1. Ask the children to choose the colour of chart paper.
2. Hand over the doilies to the children, and ask them to stick them gently on one side of the chart paper.
3. Once the doilies have dried, ask the children to wrap the gifts in them.
4. Once the gifts have been neatly packed, ask the children to tie a ribbon around the gift, and they are ready to go for the party.

Type 3:

1. Invite the children to take the poster colours such as red, green, yellow and pour them into separate bowls.
2. Help the children to use the scissors and cut the sponge into different shapes such as diyas or stars.
3. Ask them to dip the sponge into the poster colours and press it on the handmade paper.
4. Once the artwork is dry, ask the children to wrap the gift and tie it with the *mauli* to give it a traditional look.

Type 4:

1. If the gift is cylindrical, wrap the gift like a candy with frills on both the ends.
2. Invite the children to choose two colours of crepe paper, at least six to eight inches larger than the gift.
3. Now, ask the children to place the sheets one on top of the other, and place the gift on the two sheets. Now roll the gift inside the sheets.
4. Stick both the ends of the gift with the transparent tape, pinch the sheets at the corners and tie the pipe cleaner at both ends to create frills. The gift is ready to be carried in style.

Tickle the Thoughts:

1. Ask the children in what other way they can make wrapping papers.
2. Why should the gifts be wrapped?

Goals Achieved

- Enhanced association abilities
- Improved fine motor skills
- Increased social skills

Tick-tack Tip

Children may like to make envelopes or even cover diaries with these wrapping papers.

Activity–67

Headbands!

RESOURCES REQUIRED

- 8 to 10 pipe cleaners
- Beads

Getting Ready:

Keep the required resources ready.

Method:

1. Invite the children to take three pipe cleaners and help them plait the pipe cleaners together.
2. Ask them to bend the plaited pipe cleaners together such that it forms a headband. Before the children try to place the headband on their heads, ask them to cut the excess lengths of the pipe cleaners and secure the ends so that they do not hurt the children.
3. Ask them to take four to five pipe cleaners and pass half the length of the pipe cleaners through the plaited headband; fold them such that the pipe cleaners make a vertical 'V' shape.
4. Ask them to fix the beads on the headband and the 'V' shape pipe cleaners. The headbands are ready to be worn.

Tickle the Thoughts:

1. What else can be added to the headband?
2. Where else can the pipe cleaners be used?

Goals Achieved

- Enhanced association skills
- Clearer perception
- Improved fine motor skills
- Increased creativity

Tick-tack Tips:

1. You can make different patterns by sticking stickers on the headbands.
2. Children can make animal headbands by placing cloth-ears, resembling those of a rabbit, on the vertical 'V' shape pipe cleaners.

Perception

Activity–68

Personal Journal!

RESOURCES REQUIRED

- 1 sheet of card paper
- 1 can PVA glue
- 1 pair of child-safe scissors
- 1-metre-long jute rope

Getting Ready:

Keep an assortment of interesting natural objects such as leaves, twigs, feathers, wings of dead butterflies, etc., ready.

Method:

1. Invite the children to cut the card paper into equal sized pages and punch holes on each page at an equal distance so that a jute rope can pass through it till the last page, then tie a knot.
2. Ask the children to paste the collected objects on each page. Let the objects dry before the children close the personal journal.
3. Ask them to label each page and write a few sentences about the objects on them.

Tickle the Thoughts:

1. How can they use the journal daily?
2. How does writing a journal help them?

Goals Achieved

- Clearer perception
- Increased organization skills
- Exercised fine motor skills

Tick-tack Tips

1. Writing a journal helps children to keep themselves organized. Organization skill is an important life skill that needs to be put under the lens at an early age.
2. Creating a journal helps children look away from the screen. Help children find their interests and add them to the journal.

Activity–69

Stained Glass with Crayons!

RESOURCES REQUIRED

- 1 paper towel
- 1 pencil sharpener
- 1 box of crayons
- 1 black permanent marker
- A pair of child-safe scissors
- 1 hole punch
- 1 Iron
- A window
- 1 measuring tape
- 1 PVA glue

Getting Ready:

Keep a template of leaves ready for use.

Method:

1. Invite the children to measure the window panes such that the crayon-stained glass sheets fit the windows.
2. Ask them to spread out the paper towel on the work surface, and place a sheet of wax paper on top.
3. Next, ask the children to take the pencil sharpener and shave the different coloured crayons onto the wax paper.
4. Children may arrange the colours as per their choices.

5. Ask them to lay another sheet of wax paper to cover the crayon shavings.
6. Help them to set a non-steam iron to the minimum temperature and gently iron the top sheet of wax paper without tearing it.
7. The crayons will soon melt and the colour will begin to spread, forming a unique colour scheme each time they use this technique.
8. Using the PVA glue, ask the children to place the masterpiece on the windows from where the light will filter into the room!
9. The 'Stained Glass with Crayons' is ready. Enjoy the stains!

Tickle the Thoughts:

1. What is light?
2. What are colours?

Goals Achieved

- Clearer perception
- Enhanced association abilities
- Improved fine motor skills

Tick-tack Tip

Don't forget to use a large sheet of wax paper to cover the crayon shavings, as when the crayons begin to melt under the heat of the iron, there are chances that the crayon might get squeezed out and stick on the iron!

Activity–70

Kitchen Decorations!

RESOURCES REQUIRED

- 1 empty cake tin
- Steel wool
- 1 old scarf
- 10 to 12 buttons
- 1 can of PVA glue
- 1 bottle opener
- Nuts and their shells

Getting Ready:

Save kitchen junk to create funny kitchen decorations.

Method:

1. Invite the children to talk about their emotions and ask them to express their feelings by making faces using the materials.
2. Encourage them to take the cake tin to make the outline of the face.
3. You may suggest to them to place the steel wool for the hair, tie a scarf over the steel wool to give the face a warm look, and stick nuts with the PVA glue to make the eyes and the mouth. Use the bottle opener to make the nose and so on.
4. Ask the children to pass a rope through the handles of the cake tin and tie a knot to make it into a wall hanging.

Tickle the Thoughts:

1. Using the utensils, how else can we decorate the kitchen?
2. How can we add colour to the wall hangings?

Goals Achieved

- Clearer perception
- Better observation skills
- Enhanced association abilities
- Perceives the world differently

Tick-tack Tips

1. Children can make the whole body using utensils that you do not need any more.
2. Help them associate different objects to form new things that can be put to use.
3. Allow them the time to perceive things differently.

Activity–71

Stylish Window Plants!

RESOURCES REQUIRED

- 1 empty transparent bottle
- 2 plant bulbs
- 1/2 litre of water

Getting Ready:

Keep a few bulb roots that grow in water such as onions, hyacinth, etc.

Method:

1. Invite the children to fill up the bottle with water.
2. Ask the children to submerge the onion into the water with its root facing down.
3. Encourage the children to be patient and wait for the roots to grow in the water.
4. The roots will grow in water and show through the transparent glass bottle. Place the stylish plants in the kitchen's window!

Tickle the Thoughts:

1. Explain the life cycle of a plant.
2. What else does a plant need to grow?
3. Do we also have a life cycle?

Goals Achieved

- Clearer perception
- Improved sensory skills
- Better concept-building abilities

Tick-tack Tip

Grow different types of plants, depending upon the care they need. Try not to grow plants that require a lot of attention at the very beginning. Introduce the concept gradually to them.

Activity–72

Ice Candles!

RESOURCES REQUIRED

- 1 empty mineral water bottle
- 1 child-safe knife
- 15 to 20 old broken crayons
- 100 ml of water
- 2 vessels
- 6 ice cubes
- 1 candle wick
- 1 pencil and a cutter

Getting Ready:

1. Keep a set of resources for each child.
2. Pour water into a vessel and bring it to a boil.
3. Put the crayons into the second vessel and place it into the first one.
4. Wait till the crayons melt.

Method:

1. Ask the children to cut open the bottle using a child-safe knife. It should fit the size of the candle they want to make.
2. Help them make a wick by wraping a long thread around the pencil such that the thread reaches the base of the plastic bottle. Place the pencil with the wick on top of the bottle.

3. Ask them to fill the bottle with ice cubes till the top.
4. Help them pour the melted crayons into the bottle full of ice. Ensure the safety of every child since the vessel will be hot.
5. Allow it to dry.
6. Ask them to cut open the bottle, without damaging the candle inside, with the cutter. The candle is ready to be lit.

Tickle the Thoughts:

1. What was the state of crayons? Discuss different states of matter.
2. On heating, what happened that the crayons melted?
3. How do you think this texture of the candle was made?
4. Will the same thing happen if we use some other material?

Goals Achieved

- Clearer perception
- Better concept-building abilities
- Improved thinking skills
- Exercised fine motor skills

Tick-tack Tip

Children can reuse old broken candles or purchase paraffin wax to make new candles.

Activity–73

Wet Wipes!

RESOURCES REQUIRED

- 2 bowls
- 2 to 3 rolls of soft toilet paper
- 2 cups of distilled water
- 2 tbsps of liquid baby bath soap
- 1 tbsp of baby oil
- An old recyclable plastic jar
- A child-safe cutter

Getting Ready:

Keep the required resources ready.

Method:

1. Ask the children to add distilled water, liquid baby bath soap and baby oil to their mixing bowls. Mix them well.
2. Next, ask the children to place the toilet paper roll in a big bowl and pour the prepared solution on the roll.
3. Remove the inner cardboard roll from the inside of the toilet paper roll and gently pull out one end of the napkin.
4. Help the children to carefully make a small incision on the lid of the old recyclable plastic jar and pull out one end of the paper roll from the incision.

Tickle the Thoughts:

1. Ask the children if what they made, using the recyclable materials, will help them remain clean and hygienic.
2. What can they do to make the wet wipes to smell better?

Goals Achieved

- Clearer perception
- Clearer concept of self-care
- Improved sensory skills

Tick-tack Tips

1. Add some perfumed liquid baby bath soap to make the wet wipes smell good!
2. Introduce the concept of hygiene to the children with an element of fun.

Activity–74

Tepee Tents!

RESOURCES REQUIRED

- 8 to 10 bamboo garden stakes
- 6-metre-long jute rope
- Large rectangular piece of fabric such as an old bed sheet

Getting Ready:

Cut six bamboo garden stakes into equal lengths of 4 feet and 3 bamboo stakes into equal lengths of 2 feet.

Method:

1. Invite the children to tie six bamboo stakes at the top, using the jute ropes.
2. Take the 2-feet-long bamboo stakes and help children make the cross supports of the tepee frame. Secure the cross supports with jute ropes.
3. Ask the children to fix the bamboos well on the ground.
4. Tie the bedsheet around the stakes at the top, using the jute ropes again.

Tickle the Thoughts:

1. What is a shelter? What are houses?
2. Are shelters different from houses?

3. Name different types of houses.

Goals Achieved

- Clearer perception
- Improved observation skills
- Enhanced association abilities

Tick-tack Tips

1. Children can glue some feathers and contrasting fabric on the tepee tents.
2. A tepee can be put up around the child's bed to give the room a cozy-corner look.
3. Children can make tepees for their pets too.

Activity–75

Key Wind Chimes!

RESOURCES REQUIRED

- 8 to 10 metal keys
- 5-metre-long string
- 2 embroidery hoops

Getting Ready:

Make sure the keys are not rusty and are clean.

Method:

1. Invite the children to pass the string through the hole of the key and tie it to the embroidery hoop.
2. Encourage the children to hang it in a breezy place such as from the window. The keys will knock against each other and make pleasant sounds.

Tickle the Thoughts:

1. What other things can you hang instead of keys that will create pleasant sounds?
2. How does one hear sound?
3. How does sound travel?
4. What happens to sound after it is heard?

Goals Achieved

- Clearer perception
- Enhanced association abilities
- Improved sensory skills
- Increased reasoning skills

Tick-tack Tip

Children can use spoons that have a hole at top of the handle to make chimes.

Activity–76

Good Old *Firkee*!

RESOURCES REQUIRED

- 1 sheet of coloured paper
- 1 ruler
- 5 wooden sticks
- 1 PVA glue
- A pair of child-safe scissors
- 5 mapping pins
- 5 small beads
- A compass

Getting Ready:

Keep the required resources ready.

Method:

1. Invite the children to cut the coloured sheet into an 8 inch by 8 inch square.
2. Ask them to draw diagonal lines joining AC and BD, intersecting at the centre E, as shown in the figure.

Firkee

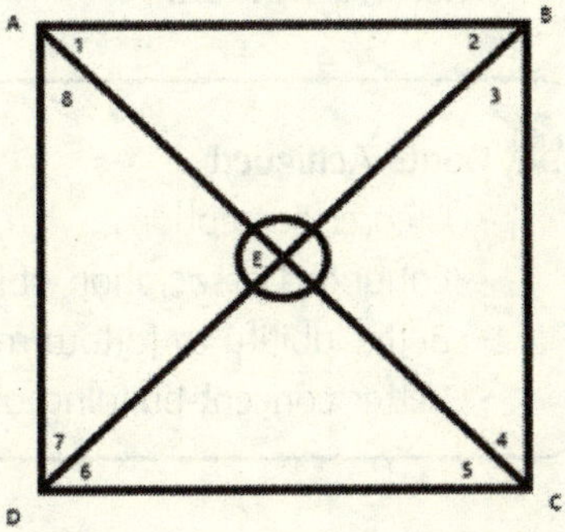

3. Ask the children to draw a circle at the centre of the square by keeping the point of the compass at E. Help them draw a circle of 1 cm radius.
4. Using the child-safe scissors, ask the children to cut the diagonals AC and BD towards the centre of each line, stopping at the marking of the circle.
5. Ask them to write numbers in an ascending order on each of the eight corners (clockwise)—from 1 to 8.
6. Now, ask the children to fold corner numbers 1, 3, 5, 7 to meet at E.
7. Then, ask the children to place a wooden stick behind the folded paper and place a small bead on the pin. Push the pin through E onto the wooden stick so that the *firkee* moves freely.

Tickle the Thoughts:

1. Once the *firkee* is ready, go outdoors with the children, line them up and ask them to run with the *firkee* in one hand at the count of three. Ask them why the *firkee* moved so fast.
2. Did the *firkee* move because they ran or was there something else? Why did their hair move when they ran?
3. What is wind?
4. What is a windmill?

Goals Achieved

- Clearer perception
- Enhanced association abilities
- Better ability to follow multiple-step instructions
- Better concept-building abilities

Tick-tack Tip

Instead of using the coloured paper, you may ask the children to colour the sheet and stick glitter before cutting the sheet for making the *firkee.*

Activity–77

Old Tee's Cushion Covers!

RESOURCES REQUIRED

- 1 t-shirt
- 1 pair of child-safe scissors
- 1 cushion
- 1 pencil

Getting Ready:

Keep some old t-shirts ready for recycling.

Method:

1. Ask the children to find some old t-shirts in their cupboards.
2. Ask them to place the cushion on the t-shirts and mark the outline of the cushion. Make another border leaving 3 cm from the outline drawn earlier. Cut the t-shirt along the outer border. Cut out the neck and the arms of the t-shirt.
3. Now, the t-shirt is two separate layers of cloth, i.e., the front and the back. Do not worry if the t-shirt has pockets. Children can use the pockets to make a design. Now, keep the cushion aside.
4. Ask the children to draw 3-cm-long lines at the edges of the t-shirt. With the help of the child-safe scissors, tell them to cut the t-shirt along these lines. The t-shirt will now have several strips at the edges.

5. Ask the children to place the cushion in between the two layers.
6. Then, ask the children to begin tying knots using the strips of the two layers at the edge of the t-shirt. The Old Tee's Cushion Covers are ready to be displayed.

Tickle the Thoughts:

1. Ask the children how they can recycle old clothes.
2. Why is recycling so important?

Goals Achieved

- Clearer perception
- Improved observation skills
- Enhanced fine motor skills

Tick-tack Tips

1. This activity gives parents the opportunity to encourage the children to reuse and recycle the resources already present in their surroundings.
2. Help the children to learn tying different types of knots. It is a good way to enhance fine motor skills.

Activity–78

Trendy Tees!

RESOURCES REQUIRED

- 1 apron
- 1 pair of rubber gloves
- 1 cotton t-shirt
- Leaves
- Plastic sheets
- 1 spray bottle
- 1 bottle of household bleach
- 1 bucket
- Paper weights or pebbles
- 1 iron

Getting Ready:

1. Keep the cotton t-shirts, according to the size of the children, ready. The t-shirts should not have any kind of print on them.
2. Go outdoors with the children to pick up some large-sized leaves from the garden.
3. Ask the children to wear their aprons and gloves.
4. Pour the household bleach into the spray bottles.

Method:

1. Invite the children to take the tees as per their sizes and slip a plastic sheet between the back and front layers of the tees.

2. Now, ask the children to press the leaf down at the place where they want to print it. Ask them to place a paper weight on top to keep the leaf from moving.
3. Then, using the spray bottle, let the children spray the bleach all around the leaf. Leave it to dry for five minutes, and in the meantime, ask the children what will happen to the tees.
4. Now, ask the children to remove the leaves and rinse the tees in water thoroughly.
5. Lastly, dry the tees in shade. To make the print permanent, iron the tees lightly.

Tickle the Thoughts:

1. What is bleach?
2. What does it do to the fabric?
3. What happens to the colour? Does the entire t-shirt turn dark or does it lose colour?

Goals Achieved

- Clearer perception
- Increased reasoning skills
- Enhanced fine motor skills

Tick-tack Tip

Children may choose to make prints on both the sides of the t-shirt, make prints on the sleeves, make scarves, cushions using the same technique.

Activity–79

Hats on!

RESOURCES REQUIRED

- 1 to 2 hats and caps
- 10 to 15 sea shells
- 3 to 4 cloth patches
- 1 pair of child-safe scissors
- 6 craft pens
- 1 can of PVA glue

Getting Ready:

Keep old hats and caps ready to use.

Method:

1. Invite the children to choose their hats or caps.
2. Ask them to stick the shells on the hats, using the glue.
3. Children may also use PVA glue to stick cloth patches on the caps.
4. They may use craft pens to write messages on their caps or even make scary designs!

Tickle the Thoughts:

1. Why do people wear hats?
2. How do hats and caps protect us?
3. If we go out in the sun for long hours without a hat, what

will happen to us?

4. What is temperature? What is the human body's correct temperature?
5. Do animals also have body temperature? Do they feel hot, cold and fall sick?
6. How can we help birds and animals in different seasons?

Goals Achieved

- Clearer perception
- Increased attention span
- Enhances empathy

Tick-tack Tips

1. Artificial flowers can be pasted on the hats to make them look pretty.
2. Along with the hats, children can even match accessories such as beach jewellery made with shells.

Activity–80

Snail's Trails!

RESOURCES REQUIRED

- 3 to 4 snails
- 1 torch
- 1 newspaper
- 1 small shovel
- 1 small glass jar
- 1 aquarium
- 1 small bunch of lettuce
- 1 stopwatch

Getting Ready:

1. During the monsoon season, step out with the children at night on a snail hunt!
2. Ask the children to wear their gumboots before stepping out!

Method:

1. Ask the children to carry their torches, shovels and small jars with them.
2. Tell them to look for snails in the garden.
3. Next, ask them to take their small shovels and carefully scoop out the mud (from under the snail) along with the snail. Place the snail into the small jar. Make sure that the snail is not hurt in any way.

4. Once back home, ask the children to gently place the snails in the aquarium and feed them lettuce.
5. Allow plenty of time to the children to observe and study the snails and their wave-like movements.
6. Now, ask the children to take their snails and place them together in one place in the aquarium and set the timer for 5 minutes. Ask them to record the distance travelled by each snail.

Tickle the Thoughts:

1. Ask them if they would like to name the snails. Will the snail be able to hear his or her name?
2. How does the snail stick so well onto the walls of the aquarium?
3. Can the snail walk on sharp surfaces too?
4. How does the snail breathe in water and on the ground?
5. What is the shell made of?

Goals Achieved

- Clearer perception
- Enhanced association abilities
- Improved sensory skills

Tick-tack-Tips:

1. Share some interesting facts about snails with the children. For example, some people eat snails and that they are a delicacy.
2. Snails can walk on razor sharp surfaces, without getting hurt.
3. They help in keeping the walls of the aquarium clean.

Activity–81

Insect's Trap!

RESOURCES REQUIRED

- 1 small plastic container
- 2 garden trowels
- 6 to 7 stones
- 2 flat and large stones
- 1 teaspoon of sugar
- 10 ml of water
- Magnifying lenses

Getting Ready:

During the day, spot a place in the garden to dig a hole.

Method:

1. Invite the children to use the garden trowel to dig a hole in the ground. The hole should be big enough for a small plastic container to sit in it.
2. Use the dug out soil to fill up the container such that the soil reaches the level of the ground.
3. To attract insects, ask the children to sprinkle some sugar and spray some water around the container to make it damp.
4. Ask the children to place a few stones around the container.
5. Leave it overnight for the insects to flock around it.
6. Ask the children to scoop out the bowl from the ground.

Tell them to study the different kinds of insects, using their magnifying lenses.

Tickle the Thoughts:

1. What are insects? Ask them to name some.
2. Why are insects important?
3. Can insects be useful for us? Name a few insects that give us things that we can use or eat.

Goals Achieved

- Clearer perception
- Enhanced association abilities
- Improved sensory skills

Tick-tack Tips

1. Encourage children to make compost for the garden.
2. Go to the library with the children to read books on insects.

Skill Development

Activity–82

De-stressing Wrist Support!

RESOURCES REQUIRED

- 1 balloon
- 1 toothpaste
- A pair of child-safe scissors

Getting Ready:

Keep the resources ready for use.

Method:

1. Ask the children to hold a balloon to their mouths.
2. Tell them to take off the cap of the toothpaste and place its nozzle into the mouth of the balloon. Squeeze about three to four tablespoons of toothpaste into the balloon.
3. Ask the children to knot their balloons carefully.
4. The 'De-stressing Wrist Support' is ready to be placed under their wrists.
5. Give them the balloons when they are about to study, or place it under their wrists when they sit in front of their computers.

Tickle the Thoughts:

1. Ask them other ways of making a wrist support.
2. What other materials give relief from similar discomforts?

Goals Achieved

- Improved sensory skills
- Exercised fine motor skills
- Increased visualization abilities

Tick-tack Tip

Children enjoy using the 'De-stressing Wrist Support' as it is very soft and cooling. Make sure that they don't get distracted and start to play with it!

Activity–83

Squeezy!

Players: 6 to 7

RESOURCES REQUIRED

- 6 to 7 balloon.
- 1 kitchen funnel
- 1 old net bag
- 200 g of starch powder in a bowl
- 1/2 litre of water
- 1 spoons
- 1 pair of child-safe scissors

Getting Ready:

Keep six to seven deflated balloons, starch powder in a mixing bowl, and water ready.

Method:

1. Invite the children to mix starch and water in a bowl to form a thick paste without lumps.
2. The paste should have a pouring consistency.

TIP: If the consistency is not achieved by mixing the solution then help them to pour the solution into a pan and bring it to a boil on a slow flame, while stirring the solution. Allow the solution to cool.

3. Help the children to fix their respective funnels at the mouths of the balloons.
4. Help them pour the solution into their balloons through the funnel. Fill only one quarter of the balloons and secure them with a knot.
5. Put each balloon inside a net bag and knot the bag as well.
6. Allow the children to play with the balloons.

Tickle the Thoughts:

1. What else can be put inside the balloon?
2. If we put water inside the balloon instead of the solution, will it still have the same effect?

Goals Achieved

- Improved sensory skills
- Enhanced fine motor skills
- Helps to de-stress
- Enhanced visualization abilities

Tick-tack Tip

Add glitter to the paste to make the activity interesting.

Activity–84

Nutella Marshmallow Slime!

RESOURCES REQUIRED

- 8 to 10 marshmallows
- 1 microwave oven
- 1 microwave-safe bowl
- 1 pair of mittens
- 2 tablespoons of Nutella
- 1 spatula

Getting Ready:

The Nutella-Marshmallow-Slime is edible. So be ready to hush elders wanting to eat the Nutella-Marshmallow-Slime!

Method:

Cooking Time: Five minutes

1. Invite the children to take eight to ten marshmallows in a microwave-safe bowl.
2. Help them place the bowl in the microwave for 25 to 30 seconds. Heat the marshmallows until they look squishy.
3. Ensure that children wear the heatproof mittens before they remove the hot bowl from the microwave.
4. Take two tablespoons of Nutella and blend it into the squishy marshmallows with the spatula.

5. The 'Nutella-Marshmallow-Slime' is ready 'not' to be served but to be played with!

Tickle the Thoughts:

1. What else can one add to this edible slime?
2. How else do you think one can make slime?
3. Can you use it for any other purpose than playing?

Goals Achieved

- Enhanced self-control
- Better sense of self-discipline
- Improved sensory skills

Tick-tack Tip

Children enjoy using the slime. Add edible sprinkles to make it look more colourful and have a different texture.

Activity–85

Banana Slime!

RESOURCES REQUIRED

- 2 ripe bananas
- 3 to 4 tablespoons of cornstarch
- 1 bowl
- 1 spoon
- 1/2 teaspoon of cinnamon powder
- 2 food colours

Getting Ready:

Keep one set of the required resources per child.

Method:

1. Invite the children to peel and mash the bananas in a bowl.
2. Help them to first add 3 tablespoons of cornstarch and blend it into the mashed bananas using a spoon. Check the consistency of the slime. If required, add more cornstarch to the mixture and blend it well until the desired consistency is achieved.
3. Ask the children to add ½ teaspoon of cinnamon powder to make the slime smell delicious.
4. Help them add food colour of their choice and once again blend in the colour. The banana-slime is ready.

Tickle the Thoughts:

1. Which fruit can replace the banana?
2. What is the property of banana that makes it an important ingredient for making slime?

Goals Achieved

- Improved sensory skills
- Exercised association abilities
- Increased visualization abilities

Tick-tack Tips

1. To add texture to the slime, children can add cloves to it.
2. Make non-edible slime by mixing one egg white with one tablespoon of liquid dish soap! Refrigerate it for 30 minutes and the slime will be ready for the jiggle!

Activity–86

Sugar Balloon Balls!

RESOURCES REQUIRED

- 150 g of sugar
- 3 balloons of different colours
- 1 bowl
- 1 pair of chopsticks
- 1 kitchen funnel
- 1 pair of child-safe scissors

Getting Ready:

Keep the required resources per child ready.

Method:

1. Ask the children to use the child-safe scissors to snip the ends of two balloons, for example, blue and green.
2. Ask them to snip the blue and green balloons at two other places.
3. Tell them to pour sugar, using the kitchen funnel, into the red balloon with no holes.
4. Ask the children to fill up the balloon half way and secure the mouth with a knot.

TIP: Use a chopstick to push the sugar into the balloon.

5. Ask the children to pull the blue balloon over the red balloon such that the knot of the red balloon is hidden inside the blue one. Do the same with the green balloon by pulling it over the blue balloon.
6. The snipped areas of the blue and green coloured balloons will be visible when the children squeeze the balloons.
7. The Sugar Balloon Balls are ready for use.

Tickle the Thoughts:

1. What else can be added to the balloons instead of sugar?
2. Ask the children what would happen if they do not snip the two balloons.
3. Would they like to add slime to the balloons?

Goals Achieved

- Improved sensory skills
- Enhanced fine motor skills
- Enhanced association abilities

Tick-tack-Tip

Children enjoy playing with textured balls, and they are good stress-busters.

Activity–87

Handmade Paper!

RESOURCES REQUIRED

- 4 egg cartons
- 1/2 litre of water
- 8″ × 8″ wire mesh
- 1 inch deep tray
- 1 blender
- Cinnamon powder
- A thin cloth napkin for each child
- 1 rolling pin
- A pair of child-safe scissors

Getting Ready:

Keep the required resources ready.

Method:

1. Ask the children to tear up the empty egg cartons.
2. Help them put the bits of egg cartons and water in a blender.
3. Add a pinch of cinnamon powder to the mixture and blend it to make a fine pulp.
4. Ask the children to place the wire mesh on the tray and pour the pulp over the wire mesh. Tell them to use their palms to squeeze out excess water.
5. Ask them to pour out the pulp into the thin cloth napkin.

Bring the ends of the napkin together and squeeze out the remaining water from the pulp.

6. Place the napkin on a flat surface and roll out the pulp into a thin sheet, using the rolling pin. This will also take care of the remaining lumps in the mixture, if any.
7. Let the pulp dry on the napkin.
8. Using the child-safe scissors, ask them to cut this paper into desired shapes and their homemade paper is ready for use.

Tickle the Thoughts:

1. What are egg cartons made of?
2. Why do we need to recycle paper?
3. How does the wastage of paper harm the environment?

Goals Achieved

- Enhanced fine motor skills
- Better observation abilities
- Helps to understand concepts such as 'reduce waste' and 'recycle the resources'
- Clearer perception

Tick-tack Tips

1. Children can make colourful handmade paper by adding a few drops of watercolour to the mixture before blending it.
2. Children can add hay, dipped in different colours, rose petals, glitter, etc., to make the handmade paper more attractive!

Activity–88

Potpourri!

RESOURCES REQUIRED

- 10 to 12 flowers
- Place to hang and dry the flowers
- 4 draw-string bags

Getting Ready:

Keep ready fragrant flowers to make potpourri with children.

Method:

1. Invite the children to choose flowers with a strong fragrance such as roses.
2. Ask them to dry the flowers completely by hanging them upside-down in a cool, airy place for a few days.
3. Ask them to take a drawstring bag and put the dried flower petals in it.
4. Ask them to add a few drops of an essential oil of their choice to the bag.
5. The potpourri is ready. Place it where the children want the fragrance to waft.

TIP: If the potpourri is in a sachet, squeeze it occasionally to release the fragrance.

Tickle the Thoughts:

1. Name flowers with strong fragrances.
2. Why does the house smell of good food? Does the cook add things that smell good?
3. Let the children explore different kinds of spices in the kitchen. Be careful with sharp objects.

Goals Achieved

- Improved sensory skills
- Enhanced observation skills
- Enhanced association abilities
- Better concept-building abilities

Tick-tack Tips

1. Potpourri can be made using different kinds of strong smelling ingredients such as:
   - Dried flowers and flower petals—Primrose
   - Herbs—Basil
   - Spices—Cinnamon and cloves
   - Roots of plants—Orris root
   - Barks—Sandalwood

   Ensure that the ingredients dry well before using them to avoid fungus and moulds, which grow in damp places.
2. Children can also dry the leaves in the oven until they are brittle but not burnt.

Activity—89

Yummy Tiaras and Crowns!

RESOURCES REQUIRED

- 1 textured greeting card
- 1 double-sided tape
- 1 pair of child-safe scissors
- 1 pair of child-safe rickrack scissors
- 1 pack of assorted candies
- Stiff cake icing in icing cones or ice-cold honey or thick starch paste to stick the candies

Getting Ready:

1. Keep the edible glue ready before the children begin to work on the tiaras and crowns.
2. Use stiff cake icing, icing cones or ice-cold honey and thick starch paste to stick the candies on the tiara to represent gems.

Method:

1. Invite children to cut strips of the textured cards long enough to fit the crown of their heads. Use the child-safe scissors. Encourage them to cut their tiaras with the help of rickrack scissors to give them a more stylish look.
2. Ask them to cut the double-sided tape and press it down at the closing point of the tiaras and crowns to hold them in place.

3. Ask the children to take the candies and stick them on their tiaras and crowns.
4. The children can pluck the candies from their tiaras and crowns and eat them while enjoying the party.

Tickle the Thoughts:

1. What are gemstones?
2. Where are gemstones found? Do they grow on trees?
3. Ask the children to name gemstones and their colours.
4. What is glue?
5. Does glue grow on trees?

Goals Achieved

- Improved sensory skills
- Enhanced association abilities
- Clearer perception
- Enhanced fine motor skills

Tick-tack Tips

1. Talk to the children about the formation of stones, rocks, fossils and gems.
2. Share some interesting facts about gems with them, such as:
   - Diamond is the hardest gemstone.
   - Amber is the softest gemstone.
   - Garnets were named after the seeds of pomegranate!

Activity–90

Grassy Grass Heads!

RESOURCES REQUIRED

- A pot
- An old pair of knitted socks
- 500 g of potting mix
- 50 g of seeds such as sprouts
- Rags
- A button
- 1 pair of googly eyes
- 1 can of PVA glue
- Paper and pencil

Getting Ready:

Save an old pair of socks.

Method:

1. Invite the children to stretch open the socks and pour the potting mix and the seeds into the sock.
2. Push the seeds and the potting mix down the sock firmly. Knot the socks to keep the contents in place. Next, put this in the pot.
3. Ask the children to use the PVA glue to stick the rags, googly eyes and a button for the nose on the pot to make a face.
4. Once in a day, ask the children to sprinkle water on the sock

and ask them to guess the kind of hairstyle each 'face' will have. Build on the curiosity by letting them touch and feel the plant grow.

5. The plants will soon grow and children will have tons of fun every day looking at the 'grassy heads'.

Tickle the Thoughts:

1. What are living things?
2. List out the properties of the living things growing on the 'Grassy Green Heads' with the children.

Goals Achieved

- Improved sensory skills
- Increased curiosity
- Enhanced association abilities
- Promotes communication skills

Tick-tack Tips

1. Children can make the 'grassy heads' using fishnet stockings too.
2. They can name their pots and role-play the characters.

Activity–91

Pompom Caps!

RESOURCES REQUIRED

- 1 ball of double-knit yarn
- 1 pair of child-safe scissors
- 1 big, pointed needle
- 1 fleece cap

Getting Ready:

Keep a ball of double-knit yarn ready.

Method:

1. Invite the children to wind the yarn carefully around their index and the tall finger. Help them to keep the yarn taut.
2. Once they have wound the yarn around their fingers 20 to 25 times, ask them to cut it at a distance of 5 cm from their fingers, holding the wrapped up yarn tightly with their thumb.
3. Pass the 5-cm-long yarn through the two fingers and tie at least two knots to secure it.
4. Now, help the child to cut the wrapped up yarn from the sides of the tall and the index fingers. You have a pompom now.
5. Brush the pompom, trimming any excess yarn sticking out. Remember not to cut the yarn that is holding the pompom together.

6. Repeat until the children get the required number of pompoms.
7. Help the children to thread a needle and tie a knot at the end of the thread.
8. Place the pompom on the cap. Help the children press it down with their thumbs and sew them. Tie two to three tight knots to secure the pompoms. Trim the excess yarn.
9. Sew the pompoms along the circumference of the cap.
10. The pompom caps are ready to be worn.

Goals Achieved

- Improved fine motor skills
- Increased attention span
- Enhanced observation abilities

Tick-tack Tip

Pompoms add a lot of colour to things that are lacklustre. If children wish to make large pompoms, ask them to use three fingers instead of two.

Activity–92

Fizzy Bath Pops!

RESOURCES REQUIRED

- 230 g of baking soda
- 115 g of cornstarch
- 115 g of mineral salts
- 115 ml of water
- 115 g of citric acid
- 10 ml of essential oil
- 28 ml of vegetable oil
- 5 drops of food colour
- 1 spoon
- 1 whisk
- 1 ice tray
- 2 bowls
- 1 weighing scale
- A pair of gloves for each child

Getting Ready:

Cover the work surface before use and ask the children to put on their gloves.

Method:

1. Invite the children to take a weighing scale and measure all the ingredients in their required quantities.

2. Ask them to take a big mixing bowl, and mix the dry ingredients.
3. Ask the children to blend the wet ingredients in a small bowl. Do not worry if the ingredients do not blend at this stage. They will blend in when the dry ingredients are added to this mixture.
4. While gently whisking the wet ingredients, add the dry ingredients to it.
5. Ask the children to press the mixture firmly into the ice trays or candy moulds.
6. Allow it to dry for a few days. Once they have dried completely, pop them out of the moulds. They are now ready to pop into the water!

Tickle the Thoughts:

1. Ask the children why it is necessary to bathe.
2. What is hygiene?
3. How do birds and animals take care of their hygiene?

Goals Achieved

- Improved sensory skills
- Enhanced attention abilities
- Increased numeracy skills
- Better concept of hygiene

Tick-tack Tips

1. To check if the ingredients are mixed well, pinch a portion from the big bowl and squeeze it to check if it clumps together. If the ingredients do not clump together, add a little bit of water and repeat the process until the ingredients clump when squeezed.
2. Alert the children before they put the fizzy bath pops into the water. They will witness the water fizzing and hear a popping sound.

Activity–93

Bug Magnets!

RESOURCES REQUIRED

- 1 can of PVA glue
- 1 clear glass stone
- 1 self-adhesive foam magnet
- A pair of googly eyes
- Glitter nail polish

Getting Ready:

Keep the required resources ready.

Method:

1. Invite the children to apply a coat of glitter nail polish on the back of a clear glass stone.
2. Allow the coat to dry before the children apply another coat of glitter nail polish to cover the base evenly. Once again, let it dry.
3. Attach the self-adhesive foam magnet at the back of the clear glass stone.
4. Flip it around and glue googly eyes on the top.
5. The Bug Magnets are ready.

Tickle the Thoughts:

1. What are bugs? Can you name a few bugs?
2. Why are bugs important?

Goals Achieved

- Enhanced fine motor skills
- Increased attention span
- Enhanced observation skills
- Enhanced association abilities

Tick-tack Tips

1. The bugs, without the magnets, can also be used as paperweights!
2. Make more bug magnets of different colours and use them at various places in the house.

Activity–94

Nail Polish Flowers!

RESOURCES REQUIRED

- 3 to 4 nail polish
- 1 jewellery wire
- 1 pair of jewellery pliers
- 1 wire cutter
- 1 pen
- 1 glass
- 5 toothpicks

Getting Ready:

1. If you do not have the required equipment, such as jewellery cutters, available at home, keep alternate options in mind.
2. Ask the children to wear aprons before they begin the activity.

Method:

1. Help the children to cut the jewellery wire to the length of 50 cm. Use the jewellery pliers to wind the wire around a pen, leaving out a piece at the top.
2. Ask the children to hold the extra wire at the top of the pen and rotate it such that the wire forms a loop.
3. Repeat the previous step to form another loop of the same size at the top of the pen.
4. Repeat the process to form three to four petals of the flower.

5. Place the flower on the toothpick and wrap the wire tightly around the toothpick to form the stem.
6. To make leaves, repeat the process of making the petals, only this time, after making the petal, pinch the petal from the top end to give it the shape of a leaf.
7. Ask the children to pour the nail paint into a mixing bowl and dip the flowers into it until they are coated fully. Allow the nail polish to settle and dry between each coat.
8. Now, place the flowers in a vase to add colour to the room!

Tickle the Thoughts:

1. Ask the children about the other uses of nail polishes.
2. In ancient times, when there were no nail polishes, how did people colour their nails?

Goals Achieved

- Improved fine motor skills
- Increased attention span
- Enhanced observation skills
- Better association abilities

Tick-tack Tip

Use different nail polishes to make a bunch of flowers, and mix shades of green and yellow to make leaves.

Activity–95

Furry Pet's Photo Booth!

Players: 1 to 2

RESOURCES REQUIRED

- 1 apron
- 1 box of poster paints
- 2 paintbrushes
- 1 cardboard box
- 1 child-safe scissors
- 1 pencil
- 1 camera
- 1 breakfast plate

Getting Ready:

1. Keep ready a cardboard box larger than the size of your pet.
2. Ask the children to wear aprons.

Method:

1. Ask the children to cut off the back of the cardboard box using the scissors. Help them unfold the top and the bottom of the box.
2. Assist the children to keep the breakfast plate at the front of

the photo booth. Ask them to draw a circle around the plate with the pencil. Remember to mark the circle at a height such that the pet is able to stick out its head comfortably from it.

3. Now, ask the children not to draw the facial features, but paint the arms, body, legs and feet of clowns, pirates, the king or queen of hearts. Allow them to dry.
4. Ask the children to take their pets to the photo booth and use their cameras to take pictures.

Tickle the Thoughts:

1. Ask the children if they love their pet.
2. How do they take care of their pet?
3. Does the pet also love them? How do they know that?

Goals Achieved

- Improved sensory skills
- Enhanced observation skills
- Improved fine motor skills
- Enhanced empathy

Tick-tack-Tip

This activity helps children to understand the importance of pets in their lives. Introduce children to the love and care that a pet needs from them. Involve the children in grooming the pet.

Activity–96

Sock-bottle Vase!

RESOURCES REQUIRED

- Newspapers
- 1 pair of gloves
- 1 apron for each child
- 1 old cotton sock
- 1 empty bottle
- 500 g of cement
- 500 ml of water
- 1 mixing bowl
- 1 spoon

Getting Ready:

1. Cover the work surface with newspaper.
2. Ask the children to wear gloves and aprons to protect themselves.

Method:

1. Ask the children to quickly go to their cupboards and bring a pair of old socks that they do not use any more.
2. Ask them to take the mixing bowl and pour 500 g of cement into it. Add water gradually while stirring the cement with a spoon. Ensure that all the lumps of cement dissolve, forming a smooth thick paste.

3. Without wasting time, ask the children to take one sock each and soak it well in the cement mix.
4. Help the children to pull up the sock onto the bottle till the neck of the bottle such that no part of the bottle is left exposed. Turn and twist the cemented sock on the bottle to give an interesting texture to the bottle.
5. Allow it to dry. Paint, if required.
6. Place a few flowers in the bottle, and the Sock-bottle Vase is ready for display!

Tickle the Thoughts:

1. Ask the children what other objects can be used for recycling.
2. How else can they decorate the Sock-bottle Vase?

Goals Achieved

- Improved sensory skills
- Enhanced association abilities
- Clearer perception

Tick-tack Tips

1. Crumpling long stockings leaves an interesting texture.
2. Children may recycle old, worn-out, high shoes using the same technique.

Activity–97

Jiggle Balloon Heads!

RESOURCES REQUIRED

- 4 to 5 large balloons without any prints
- 250 g flour
- 1 pair of chopsticks
- 1 kitchen funnel
- 10 wiggly eyes
- Stickers with facial expressions

Getting Ready:

Keep the required resources ready.

Method:

1. Ask the children to take one balloon at a time, inflate and then deflate them so that the latex of the balloon stretches well.
2. Ask them to push the kitchen funnel into the mouth of the balloon.
3. Help them spoon in the flour through the funnel into the balloon.
4. Fill half of the balloon with flour and then tie a knot.
5. Place the stickers on the balloons and stick wiggly eyes to finish the 'Jiggle Balloon Heads'.

Tickle the Thoughts:

1. Organize a role-play session and ask the children to name the characters played by their teammates.
2. Ask the children to draw facial expressions on the balloons.

Goals Achieved

- Increased communication skills
- Enhanced emotional skills
- Improved sensory skills
- Enhanced association abilities

Tick-tack Tip

Children enjoy poking and squeezing balloons. Allow them to use different colours to express their emotions. They can make them more expressive by making red spots to show anger or frustration.

Activity–98

Quick Trick for Stuffy Nose!

RESOURCES REQUIRED

- 6 tablespoons of vapour rub
- 3 cups of cornstarch
- 3 tablespoons of water
- 2 ice trays
- 1 cup of hot water

Getting Ready:

Ensure that the children wear gloves before they begin the activity.

Method:

1. Ask the children to mix the vapour rub and cornstarch in a mixing bowl with a spoon.
2. Help them to slowly add water to the mixture and knead it into small balls.
3. Ask them to take the ice trays and push each ball into the ice tray.
4. Refrigerate for 30 minutes and pop out the vapour-cornstarch cubes from the ice trays.
5. Help the children to take one cube in a bowl and pour a cup of steaming hot water.

6. The hot water will melt the cube and the smell of the vapour will spread in the room. This will help to get rid of a stuffy nose.

Tickle the Thoughts:

1. Explain to the children how the smell of the vapour spreads in the room.
2. What are gases? Can you name a few?
3. How else can you help yourself when you fall ill?

Goals Achieved

- Enhanced self-help skills
- Promotes self-care
- Improved sensory skills
- Better concept-building abilities

Tick-tack Tips

1. Parents may use this activity to help children work on their self-help skills.
2. You may encourage the children to be independent and take care of themselves, but watch over them without the children realizing it.

Activity–99

Funny Cupcakes!

RESOURCES REQUIRED

- 500 g of cake icing
- Cupcake for every child
- 2 icing cones
- 2 different food colours
- Spoons and plates to serve
- Food decorations such as edible gems, M&Ms, fruits for all the children

Getting Ready:

Keep plenty of cupcakes and food decorations ready.

Method:

1. Help the children mix icing sugar and water in a bowl. Ensure that the mixture does not have lumps.
2. Ask the children to add one or two drops of food colour of their choice and pour the icing into the icing cones.
3. Ask them to squeeze the icing from the cone onto the cupcakes.
4. Add the decorations to the icing. Let the children decide what they want to make on the cupcakes. Help them make the face of a snowman or that of Santa Clause!

Tickle the Thoughts:

1. What else can they add to the cupcakes to have some more fun?
2. What would they like to make—some wiggly insects, funny looking Uncle Sam or a spooky Halloween ghost to scare the friends around?

Goals Achieved

- Improved sensory skills
- Promotes culinary skills
- Enhanced association abilities

Tick-tack Tip

You can add edible gems like M&Ms, fruits, scoops of ice cream to add more colour and fun to the cupcakes.

Activity–100

Raffia Envelopes!

RESOURCES REQUIRED

- 1/4 sheet of coloured handmade paper
- A pair of child-safe scissors
- Raffia or flexible dry leaves
- 1 hole punch
- 1 transparent tape
- 1 envelope
- 1 can of PVA glue

Getting Ready:

Keep the required resources ready for the children.

Method:

1. Help the children draw a basic shape, such as a star, on the handmade paper and cut it out using child-safe scissors.
2. Ask them to punch a hole at the centre of the star using the hole punch.
3. Tie a knot at one end of the raffia leaf and from the centre of the star; ask them to begin threading the raffia around it.
4. Secure the star on the envelope with the help of the glue. The 'Raffia Envelopes' are ready for use.

Tickle the Thoughts:

1. What is raffia?
2. Ask the children what else they can use in place of raffia.

Goals Achieved

- Improved fine motor skills
- Enhanced attention span
- Increased observation skills
- Enhanced association abilities

Tick-tack Tips

1. Children can draw, cut out papers and thread the outline of a *kalash* (an earthen pot with a coconut and mango leaves used on auspicious occasions) using the holy thread, called *mauli*, worn by Hindus, to make envelopes.
2. Secure the ends of the raffia by twisting and securing them with a transparent tape such that this pointy end easily passes through the hole made on the handmade paper.

Activity–101

Selfie Props!

RESOURCES REQUIRED

- 1 pair of wooden chopsticks per prop
- 1 sheet of coloured card paper
- Cotton
- PVA glue
- 5 pencils
- 1 pair of child-safe scissors

Getting Ready:

Keep the required resources ready.

Method:

1. Help the children draw interesting shapes such as moustaches, beards, huge sunglasses on the coloured card paper, and ask them to cut them out using child-safe scissors.
2. Ask them to use glue to stick cotton on the beard to turn it into a funny prop.
3. Help children to make funny sunglasses. Ask them to cut a table tennis ball into half. Next, urge them to use PVA glue to stick springs on each half. They must stick the springs on the concave side of the halves. On the convex side of the ball, they may stick the googly eyes. Now, ask them to stick

the 'spring-eyes' on the sunglasses!

4. To make the arms of the sunglasses, ask the children to stick the chopsticks on either ends of the sunglasses.
5. Make each of them wear the props they have made.
6. Now, give them a camera and let them click selfies to make fond memories!

Tickle the Thoughts:

1. What is a camera?
2. What are concave and convex lenses?
3. How does the camera work?
4. How does the camera change its direction to take selfies?
5. Do the pictures help us in preserving fond memories? Pull out an album and share fond memories with them!

Goals Achieved

- Improved fine motor skills
- Increased attention span
- Enhanced association abilities
- Better concept of photography

Tick-tack Tips

1. In the present day scenario, where children are getting addicted to mobiles, this activity will keep them away from the gadgets and introduce them to yet another world of photography. This activity is a sure shot way of introducing them to photography using cameras.

2. Parents may take the children to a photographer's studio to see how photographs were developed before the mobiles with cameras came in.

Conclusion!

The present generation of children squanders too much time watching television and using gadgets. This, undoubtedly, has led to major health concerns and behavioural issues. While we know that televisions and computers are sources of knowledge, it is important for us to remember that it is only a second-hand source of information when compared to experiencing knowledge by doing certain things. Taking children away from the screen is the new challenge the present parenting generation is facing.

Parenting is hard and is often unpredictable. The external pressures to over achieve and recklessly spend beyond their means have adverse effects on children, which adds unwanted pressure. What is threatening to a child is precisely the elevated pressure that is not visible to many. The profound effects of disharmony, abuse, unutterable loneliness and domestic violence are invariably the hidden monsters that threaten children. These colossal pressures on a child can disable the meaningful relationships and the bonds parents share with their children and vice versa. It harms the essential unity and disrupts the possible communication between the families. When the going gets tough, parents need to slow down and rebuild their bond with children. They need to lead from the front. Home is the most essential crossroads in a child's life. Parents need to ensure that children continuously hear about motivational and inspirational people that the child is capable of taking after. *Being a Creative Genius* will help parents escort the child away from gadgets. It will provide ample opportunities for the concerned parents to nurture creative thinking in their child.

Moreover, as you proceed from activity to activity in this book, you will discover the innate strengths your child has, which, until now, were suppressed under mounting pressures of various sorts. You will be able to initiate healthy conversations. 'Tickle the Thoughts' is tailor-made for your creative and fun-filled conversations with your child. It will help him or her to become 'creatively-gifted'. The inspired and motivated child will instantly discover his or her 'creative-self'. The child will seek solutions to problems with a broader understanding and strive to excel in the world with a modern perspective. In your creative journey, you will gain opportunities to know the hidden potentials your child naturally possesses and those when nurtured, can develop into their strengths.

We desperately set unrealistic targets of creating a problem-free world. Are these targets required? Each generation will inevitably encounter a new set of problems. So how do we help our children today to fight this?

When we empower our children with creativity, we will empower them to construct a 'solution-rich' world. They will be flexible, non-judgemental, creative and constructive to refocus their attention from 'what-if' to 'what-can-be' and create a new road-map to a worthier world.